CW01668063

Live the City

Welcome

Inspired by our own travels, we founded Live The City in 2005 to create a range of guides which make sightseeing fun. We are passionate about exploring new places, uncovering hidden treasures and discovering those little stories which make us think, "Hmmm! I never knew that!".

Our Oxford guide is the perfect way to explore this 'city of dreaming spires' and learn about the world famous University, centuries of incredible history and the relationship between 'Town and Gown'.

Have a great time and please do let us know how you get on, we'd love to hear from you.

Best wishes,

Robin Melody

Robin Freebairn and Melody White, Founders of Live The City

www.livethecity.com

Contents

Author: Melody Brooker

Additional Material: Angela White, Jennie Binks and Deborah Robinson

Editor: Robin Freebairn

With thanks to Felicity Tholstrup, Hidden Oxford and Anneke Bambery, Bodleian Library.

Original Photography: Robin Freebairn

The following images are reproduced by kind permission of the copyright holder as indicated: Page 34 (centre) Theo Jacobs; Page 43 (lower) Greg Smolonsid/Photovibe; Page 54 (centre) – Mark Bassett, Oxford Castle Unlocked; Page 56 (title and bottom left) Ashmolean Museum, University of Oxford ; Page 58 (lower) – Blenheim Palace.

Published in Great Britain by Live The City Publishing.

Production: Labute Group

* Live The City guide to Cambridge – Best Tourism Experience – East of England regional winner – enjoy England Awards for Excellence 2009.

We would be delighted to receive your feedback. Drop us a line to **hello@livethecity.com**

ISBN: 978-0-9562438-2-9

www.livethecity.com

FSC Mixed Sources
Product group from well-managed forests and other controlled sources
Cert no. TT-COC-002755
www.fsc.org
© 1996 Forest Stewardship Council

PEFC
PEFC/16-33-997

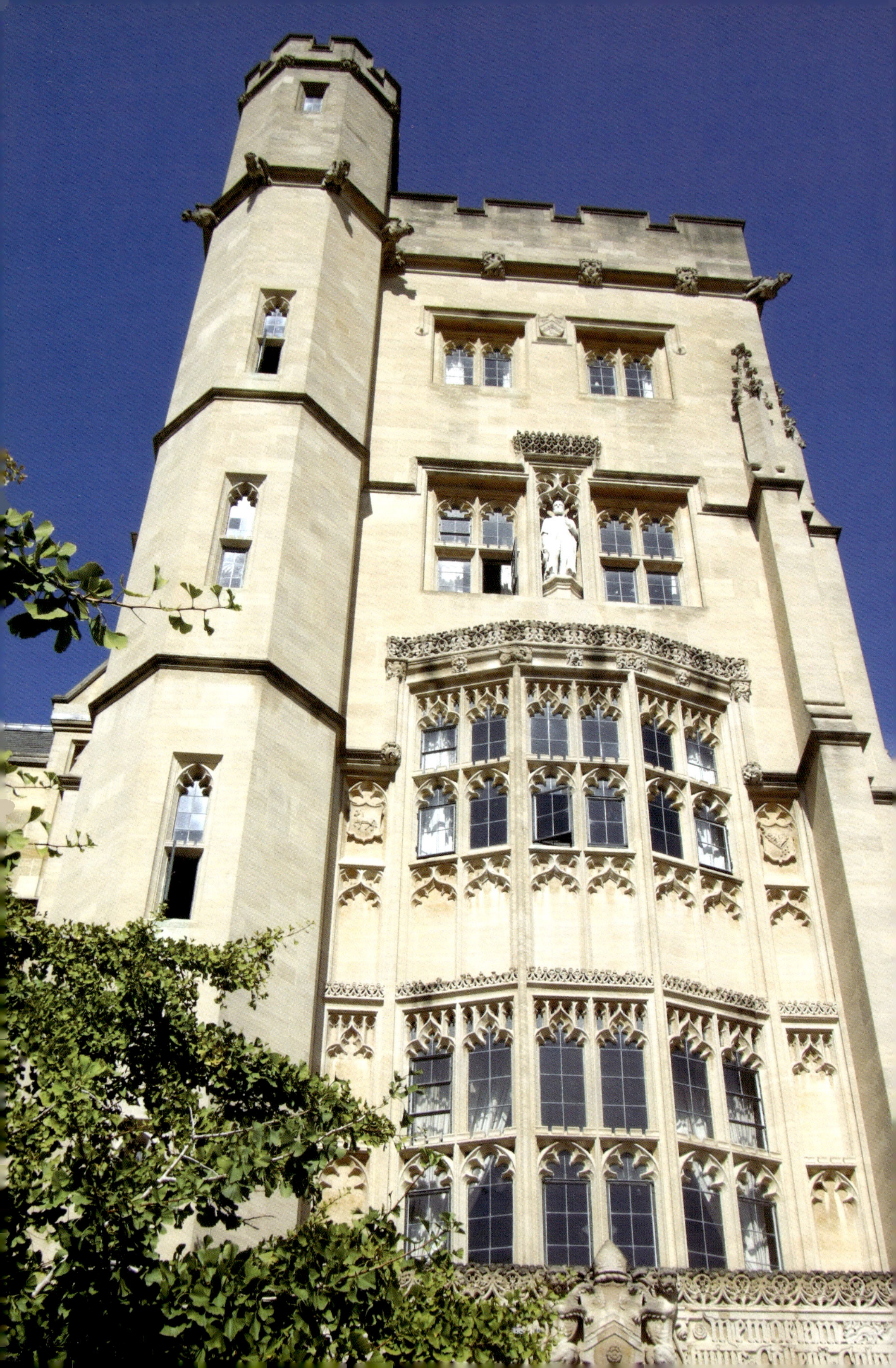

EXPLORE

Oxford is a beautiful city with lots of fascinating sights to explore. This guidebook contains two step-by-step sightseeing trails to help you see the very best of the city during your visit.

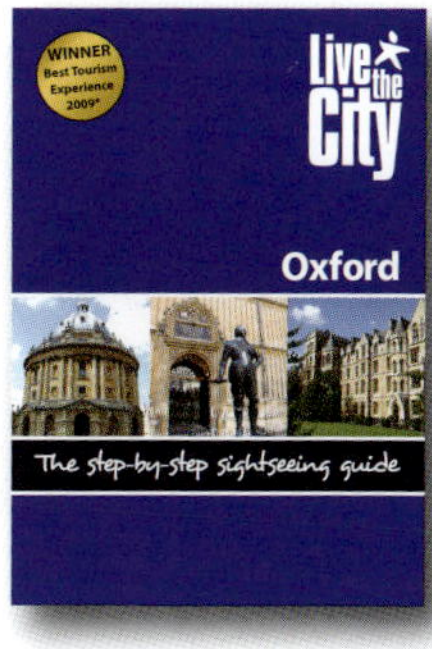

SOLVE

As part of our award winning sightseeing format, you'll see that our trails also include a series of clues for you to solve as you explore. These brainteasers will help you to discover more and add a little something extra to your sightseeing experience.

PLAY

When you've finished sightseeing, visit our website **www.livethecity.com** to play the free quiz based on the clues you've solved. Everyone who plays the quiz has a chance to win a cash prize. Good luck!

Three steps to help make the most of your visit.

A Brief History

The waterways through Oxford were vital trade arteries

The earliest recorded settlement on what is now known as Oxford was during Saxon times. The name for this settlement was Oxenaforda, meaning 'The Ford of the Ox'.

Whilst there are several possible founders of the town, the most commonly held theory relates to St Frideswide, the daughter of an Anglo Saxon king. Born in around 659, in early life, the young princess founded a priory and it was this settlement which formed the basis of Oxford. St Frideswide Priory existed until 1002 when it was destroyed in a fire blamed on the invading Danes.

Later that century, the settlement was invaded again, this time by the Normans in 1066. After this invasion, the Norman nobleman Robert D'Oilly became governor of Oxford and built the castle and protective wall around the town. Parts of this wall remain today at St Michael at the Northgate. From the 12th century, Oxford's excellent links with other trading towns via its well connected waterways saw the town emerge as an important centre of trade in wool and cloth.

As Oxford grew in size and importance, a number of small monasteries and religious orders were established in the town. Each of these institutions provided religious education for its inhabitants. The first scholars educated within monasteries went to Paris to finish their education. In 1167, following a dispute with the French, Henry II cut ties with France. As a result, these scholars returned and settled in Oxford, founding a number of 'Halls' which provided lodging and education.

Parts of the ancient city wall

Christ Church Cathedral, site of St Frideswide's Priory

The Swindlestock was the site of many 'town and gown' riots

During the 13th century, the rapid growth of the University began to take its toll on the lives of the townsfolk. Great parts of Oxford were demolished to make way for new college buildings and a gulf developed between the privileged lives of the University members and the townsfolk, leading to frequent riots between the two groups. By the mid 14th century, the majority of the townsfolk were living in extreme poverty, conditions made worse by the arrival of the Black Death which left hundreds dead.

Over the course of the next 200 years, the University continued to flourish and grow, firmly entrenched in its tradition of educating England's aristocracy and strengthening its links with royalty.

The mid 16th century saw turbulent times for Oxford and indeed, the country. In 1536, Henry VIII's parliament ordered the dissolution of the monasteries as he turned his back on the Catholic faith. Since the University was primarily a religious institution, it too became a target and was spared only due to Henry's own love of education. The various religious Halls which had been so prominent in the medieval University were broken up and absorbed by the colleges.

The Protestant Reformation continued under the rule of Henry's son, Edward VI. The first Book of Common Prayer was published in 1549 and church services began to be conducted in English. This period of enlightenment was however short-lived. Upon Edward's death in 1553, his half sister, Mary I came to the throne. She immediately set to work to return England to Catholicism. During her reign, 'Bloody Mary' as she became known, tried and executed some 300 Protestants for acts of heresy. Many of these trials were held in Oxford at St Mary's Church, most famously, those of the Oxford Martyrs', Hugh Latimer, Nicholas Ridley and Thomas Cranmer.

Henry VIII seized control of Christ Church

The Church of St Mary the Virgin

Magdalen Tower was used as a look out against Parliamentarian forces

Less than a century later, Oxford was once again to find itself at the centre of political upheaval. During the English Civil War, the University's strong allegiance to the crown made it a safe haven for Royalists including King Charles I who took refuge at Christ Church. In keeping with their traditionally opposing views, the townsfolk took the side of Cromwell's army, causing yet more skirmishes between 'town' and 'gown'.

The remainder of the 17th century saw further expansion of the University with the building of some of its most iconic landmarks including the Radcliffe Camera. Sadly, these architectural efforts were not mirrored in the efforts of the students. Academic performance hit an all time low and students became known for their debauched lifestyles rather than their scholarly achievements.

Meanwhile, the city was enjoying a period of renewed prosperity, with the arrival of the Oxford Canal and the Oxford University Press, both bringing industry and new jobs to the townsfolk. The city limits grew to incorporate the new housing required to accommodate the increasing workforce, Jericho being a good example of this.

The 19th century brought several improvements to the lives of Oxford inhabitants. Gas lighting was introduced in 1819, a railway line to London was built in 1844, two hospitals were opened, and, by the 1880s, everyone in Oxford had a piped water supply.

Educational standards improved greatly during the 19th century as University officials restored a greater sense of morality and duty within their students. The first women's colleges, Lady Margaret Hall and Somerville, were established in 1879, although it was not until 1920 that women were accepted as members of the University.

The Radcliffe Camera

Lady Margaret Hall

The Oxford University Press

Great changes were also afoot in Oxford's industrial landscape. At the turn of the century, in 1903, the Frank Cooper Jam Factory opened, followed by William Morris' Motor Company in 1910. By the 1930s, Oxford was a major manufacturing centre. The city was fortunate to escape any serious damage during the Second World War. Supposedly, this was because Hitler admired the city and had ambitions to make Oxford the new capital once he had won the war!

Oxford in the 21st century is a beautiful and fascinating city with a rich and varied history. With so much to explore and discover, it is little wonder that more than 9 million people from across the globe visit the city each year.

The Oxford Garage

One of the many visitor hotspots in Oxford

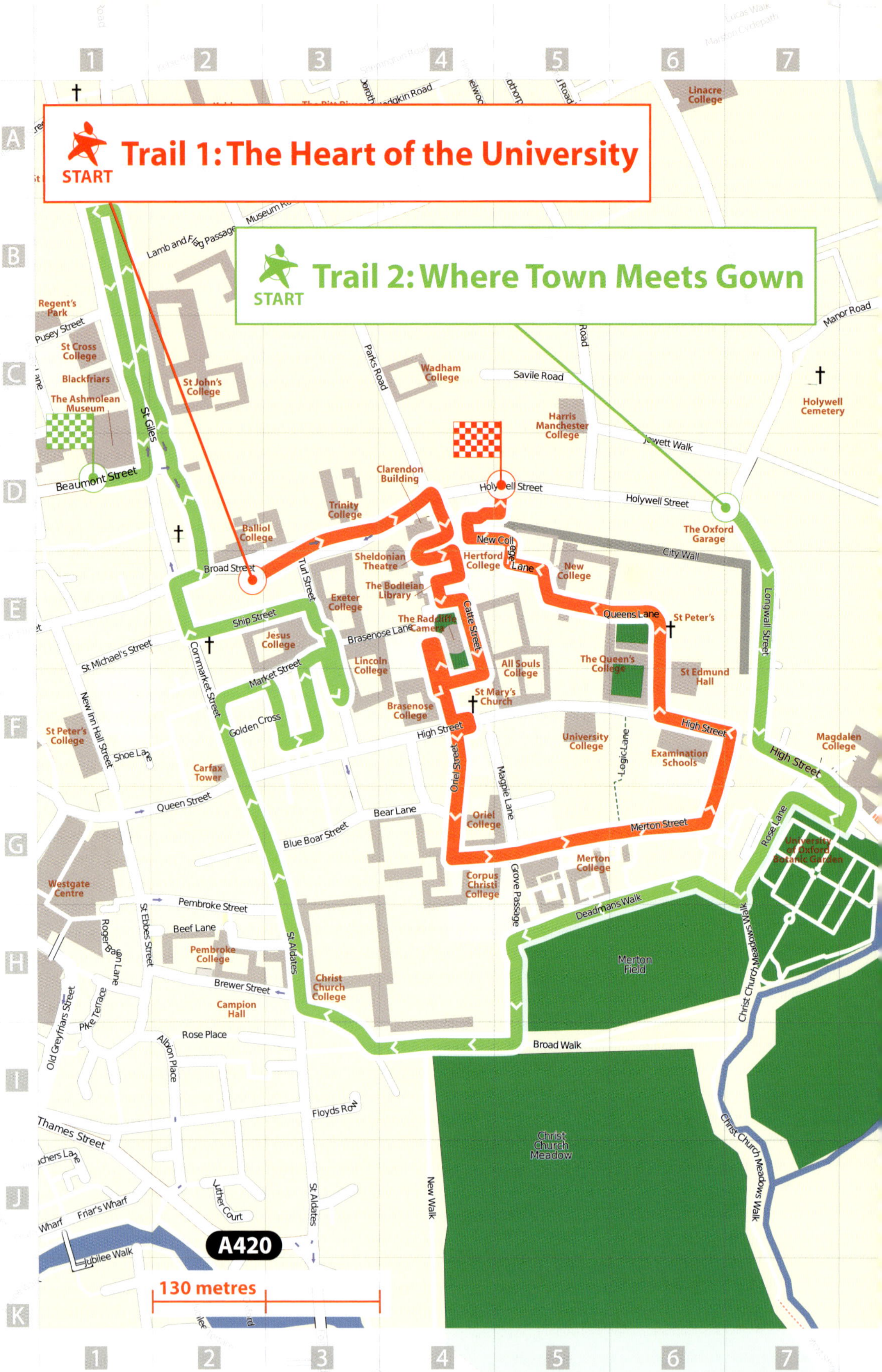
Trail 1: The Heart of the University
START
Trail 2: Where Town Meets Gown
START
Linacre College
Regent's Park
Pusey Street
St Cross College
Blackfriars
The Ashmolean Museum
St Giles
Beaumont Street
Lamb and Flag Passage
Museum Road
St John's College
Parks Road
Wadham College
Savile Road
Harris Manchester College
Jowett Walk
Holywell Cemetery
Manor Road
Clarendon Building
Holywell Street
Trinity College
Balliol College
Broad Street
The Oxford Garage
New College Lane
City Wall
Sheldonian Theatre
Hertford College
New College
Turl Street
The Bodleian Library
Exeter College
Longwall Street
Ship Street
Jesus College
Brasenose Lane
The Radcliffe Camera
Catte Street
Queens Lane
St Peter's
St Michael's Street
Cornmarket Street
Market Street
Lincoln College
All Souls College
The Queen's College
St Edmund Hall
St Mary's Church
Brasenose College
High Street
Golden Cross
St Peter's College
New Inn Hall Street
Shoe Lane
University College
Logic Lane
Examination Schools
Magdalen College
Carfax Tower
Queen Street
Oriel Street
Magpie Lane
Bear Lane
Blue Boar Street
Oriel College
Merton Street
Rose Lane
University of Oxford Botanic Garden
Westgate Centre
Merton College
Corpus Christi College
Grove Passage
Pembroke Street
St Ebbes Street
St Aldates
Deadmans Walk
Beef Lane
Roger Bacon Lane
Pembroke College
Merton Field
Christ Church College
Brewer Street
Old Greyfriars Street
Pike Terrace
Campion Hall
Christ Church Meadows Walk
Rose Place
Albion Place
Broad Walk
Floyds Row
Thames Street
Christ Church Meadow
Friar's Wharf
Luther Court
New Walk
Jubilee Walk
A420
130 metres
1 2 3 4 5 6 7
A B C D E F G H I J K

Trail 1: The Heart of the University

This fascinating trail covers the central hub of the University and is packed full of iconic landmarks and historic highlights. Explore the wonders of the Bodleian Library, admire the architectural eccentricity of the Radcliffe Camera and take in many of the most famous University Colleges.

Start: Oxfam, Broad Street.

Finish: Bath Place.

Highlights:

- The Bodleian Library
- Radcliffe Camera
- The Sheldonian Theatre
- The University Church
- New College

Trail Time: allow around 1 hour 30 minutes

Distance: approximately 1.3 miles

No. of Clues: 11

Trail 2: Where Town Meets Gown

This trail is a perfect blend of 'town and gown'. Stroll through the tranquil riverside grounds of Magdalen College and neighbouring Botanic Garden. Explore the world of Christ Church College which inspired Alice's Wonderland. Learn tales of the tragic Oxford Martyrs and of the ferocious town vs gown riots.

Start: The Oxford Garage, corner of Holywell Street and Longwall Street.

Finish: The Ashmolean Museum, Beaumont Street.

Highlights:

- Christ Church College
- Botanic Garden
- The Ashmolean Museum
- Magdalen College
- The Covered Market
- The Eagle and Child Pub

Trail Time: allow around 2 hours

Distance: approximately 2 miles

No. of Clues: 10

Trail 1: The Heart of the University
START
1
2
3
4
5
6
7
A
B
C
D
E
F
G
H
I
J
K
Linacre College
Rhodes House and Gardens
Lamb and Flag Passage
Museum Road
Mansfield College
Mansfield Road
St Cross Road
Manor Road
Regent's Park
Pusey Street
St Cross College
Blackfriars
The Ashmolean Museum
St John's College
Parks Road
Wadham College
Savile Road
Harris Manchester College
Jowett Walk
Holywell Cemetery
St Giles
Beaumont Street
Clarendon Building
Trinity College
Holywell Street
The Oxford Garage
Balliol College
Broad Street
New College Lane
Hertford College
Sheldonian Theatre
New College
City Wall
Turl Street
The Bodleian Library
Exeter College
Longwall Street
Queens Lane
St Peter's
Ship Street
The Radcliffe Camera
Catte Street
Brasenose Lane
Jesus College
St Michael's Street
Cornmarket Street
Market Street
Lincoln College
All Souls College
The Queen's College
St Edmund Hall
St Mary's Church
Brasenose College
High Street
New Inn Hall Street
Golden Cross
St Peter's College
Shoe Lane
University College
Logic Lane
Examination Schools
Magdalen College
Oriel Street
Magpie Lane
Carfax Tower
Queen Street
Bear Lane
Oriel College
Merton Street
Rose Lane
Blue Boar Street
University of Oxford Botanic Garden
Merton College
Corpus Christi College
Grove Passage
Westgate Centre
Pembroke Street
Deadman's Walk
St Ebbes Street
Beef Lane
Rogers Bacon Lane
Pembroke College
St Aldates
Merton Field
Christ Church Meadow Walk
Brewer Street
Christ Church College
Old Greyfriars Street
Pike Terrace
Campion Hall
Albion Place
Rose Place
Broad Walk
Floyds Row
Thames Street
Christ Church Meadow
Preachers Lane
New Walk
Christ Church Meadows Walk
Luther Court
Friar's Wharf
Jubilee Walk
A420
130 metres

Trail 1

The Heart of the University

This fascinating trail covers the central hub of the University and is packed full of iconic landmarks and historic highlights. Explore the wonders of the Bodleian Library, admire the architectural eccentricity of the Radcliffe Camera and take in many of the most famous University Colleges.

Start: Oxfam, Broad Street.

Finish: Bath Place.

Highlights:

- The Bodleian Library
- Radcliffe Camera
- The Sheldonian Theatre
- The University Church
- New College

Trail Time: allow around 1 hour 30 minutes

Distance: approximately 1.3 miles

No. of Clues: 11

Let's get started…

Oxfam to Balliol College

Oxfam

The world's first Oxfam Shop

Begin outside the Tourist Information Centre on Broad Street. To the right is the Oxfam charity shop.

This Oxfam shop was opened in 1947 and is the first of its kind. The international aid charity Oxfam began here in Oxford in 1942. Originally known as the Oxford Committee for Famine Relief, the first official meeting of the group was held in St Mary's Church. The committee's first mission was to persuade the British Government to allow food supplies through Allied blockades to the starving citizens of occupied Greece. Today, the charity works in over 100 countries to provide support for victims of poverty. The head office of Oxfam Great Britain remains in Oxford.

Clue 1. Which qualities is Cecil remembered for?

Balliol College

Cross Broad Street to the main entrance of Balliol College.

Balliol was founded in 1263, making it one of three colleges which claim to be the oldest in Oxford. The college enjoys a reputation as one of the wealthiest and best performing within the University although this has not always been the case. Balliol began its rise from centuries of poverty and obscurity under the guidance of 19th century master, Benjamin Jowett. Jowett's reforms were based on the principle that students should not simply be taught facts, but also be educated to live good lives. His methods proved extremely successful and under his influence, the college began to enjoy a new period of high academic achievement which continues to this day.

Balliol is considered to be one of the most progressive colleges and has long been known for its liberal political views. The college accepts a high proportion of students from state schools and has abolished many ancient traditions including the wearing of gowns and saying Grace before dinner.

Balliol College

Trinity College

The grounds of Trinity College

Continue along the left hand side of Broad Street to a large pair of iron gates.

Trinity College is one of the University's most visited colleges, its beautiful grounds, visible through the iron gates proving a popular attraction for visitors. Despite its extensive grounds, the college has only 400 students, making it one of the smallest within the University.

Trinity was founded in 1555 on the site of the former Durham College, an establishment founded in 1286 by the monks of Durham Abbey. After Henry VIII's dissolution of the monasteries, the college was re-founded by Sir Thomas Pope. Pope had no surviving children and felt that by founding the college, he would be leaving a lasting legacy to ensure his name would not be forgotten. Life for Trinity's scholars in the 16th century was hard. The daily schedule began with a 5am mass, followed by an hour long lecture in philosophy. Breakfast would be followed by three hours of theological debates in the chapel. Lunch would be taken in silence whilst the bible was read aloud and finally, the remainder of the day would be taken up with lectures in Latin or Greek. Things are a little more relaxed for today's students.

The Angel of the Broad

Before moving on, turn your gaze upwards to the rooftop of Blackwell's Art Shop.

Here stands the newest addition to Oxford's skyline, the Anthony Gormley Bronze, which was donated to nearby Exeter College in May 2009. The statue has already earned the local nickname The Angel of the Broad.

Continue along the left hand side of Broad Street to the White Horse Pub.

The White Horse Pub appears regularly in episodes of the detective series *Inspector Morse* and its spin-off, *Lewis*.

Clue 2. Commemorated at The White Horse, a riot between which two football clubs made Billy a hero?

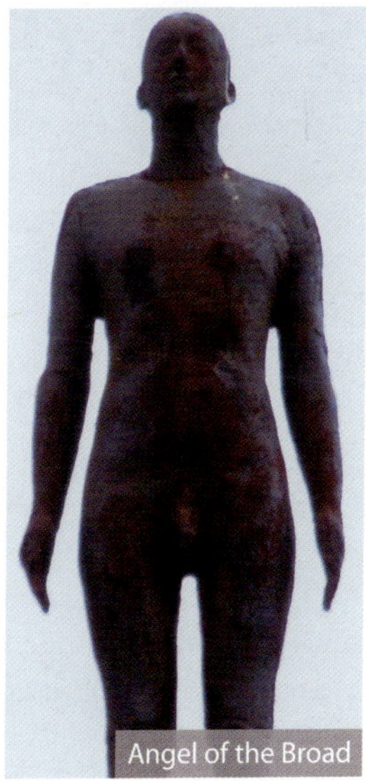
Angel of the Broad

Blackwell's Bookshop to The Museum of the History of Science

Blackwell's Bookshop

Blackwell's Bookshop

If open, make your way inside Blackwell's Bookshop.

Now part of an international publishing empire, Blackwell's first opened its doors here on Broad Street in 1879. Proprietor Benjamin Henry Blackwell's original shop was just 12ft (3.6m) square and could only accommodate three customers at any one time. Despite the cramped conditions, Benjamin's passion for books earned him respect amongst the University scholars and masters and gradually, he was able to expand his business.

The Norrington Room

To visit The Norrington Room, make your way down the internal staircase.

In 1966, the underground Norrington Room, named after the then President of Trinity College, was opened. This vast room expands to an area of approximately 10,000sq ft beneath the pretty Lavender Garden of Trinity College and is thought to be the largest space devoted to book sales in the whole of Europe.

The Museum of the History of Science

The Museum of the History of Science

Leave Blackwell's and cross Broad Street to The Museum of The History of Science.

The Museum of the History of Science is a fascinating collection of scientific artefacts and exhibits housed within beautiful surroundings. The museum, also known as The Old Ashmolean, was built between 1678 and 1683 by the University to house the Tradescant Collection. This remarkable collection of curiosities was compiled by John Tradescant and his son, also John during the 17th century. John Tradescant the younger left the collection to his friend Elias Ashmole who later donated it in its entirety to the University. The Old Ashmolean is believed to have been the first public museum within Europe.

Inside, look out for the incredible Bladder Fish dating from the 17th century and the blackboard and chalk used by Einstein during a visit to Oxford in 1931.

The Emperors' Heads

One of the Emperors' Heads

Leave the Museum and turn right.

The 17 stone heads which surround the Sheldonian Theatre are known as 'The Emperors' Heads' or 'The Bearded Ones'. The original heads were installed upon the theatre's completion in 1669 and were replaced 200 years later. Unfortunately, the second incarnation of these stately gentlemen was in a poor quality stone which was quickly eroded by the weather.

In 1972, local sculptor Michael Black was tasked with creating 17 new heads which are the ones you see today. No-one knows who or what the heads were intended to symbolise, although the most popular theory is that they depict the history of beards!

The Clarendon Building

Follow the line of 'Emperors' to the steps leading to the main entrance to the Clarendon Building.

The Clarendon Building was constructed between 1711 and 1713 to house the Oxford University Press which had previously occupied part of the Sheldonian Theatre.

The building is named in honour of the English historian and statesman, Sir Edward Hyde, the first Earl of Clarendon.

Hyde's most famous achievement was to write The History of the Rebellion and Civil Wars in England. The book became a best seller of its time and the proceeds were used to fund the construction of this building.

The Oxford University Press moved to much larger premises on Walton Street in 1832. Today, the Clarendon Building is home to administrative offices of the University.

The Clarendon Building

Clue 3. What is this figure holding in her hand?

The Sheldonian Theatre to Hertford College

The Sheldonian Theatre

The Sheldonian Theatre

Turn right into Catte Street and continue to the main entrance to The Sheldonian Theatre via the large iron gates on the right.

The Sheldonian Theatre was built between 1664 and 1668 as a fitting location for the ceremonial services of the University. Degree ceremonies are held here to this day along with regular concerts and lectures.

The Sheldonian was commissioned in 1662 by the then Chancellor of Oxford University, Gilbert Sheldon. This prestigious project was awarded to a young architect in the early stages of his career, a 30 year old Christopher Wren.

Wren's designs broke with the fashions of the time to follow a more classical design based on the open air Theatre of Marcellus in Rome. A roof was sensibly added to accommodate the less favourable Oxfordshire climate! The ingenious design for the roof meant that no internal pillars were required for support. The result is that none of the 2,000 strong audience has a restricted view of the action.

Hertford College

Leave the grounds of The Sheldonian and return to Catte Street. Directly ahead is The Bridge of Sighs.

Hertford Bridge, more commonly referred to as The Bridge of Sighs, was built in 1913 to connect the Old and New Quadrangles of Hertford College.

Hertford College began life as Hart Hall in 1282, providing lodgings for students and fellows of the University. The site grew in size over the coming centuries and after several periods of financial hardship, was re-founded and granted full college status as Hertford College in 1874 after a large donation by Sir Thomas Baring.

The author Evelyn Waugh was an undergraduate at Hertford. By his own admission, Waugh neglected his studies whilst at Oxford, devoting the majority of his time to writing. He did however embrace the social side of University life with gusto. When asked in later life whether he had competed in any college sports, he replied "I drank for Hertford". The author's time at Hertford provided much of the inspiration for his most famous novel, *Brideshead Revisited*.

The Bridge of Sighs

Clue 4. It is a matter of Principal to find the man who 'bridges' Old and New at Hertford. Who was he?

The Bodleian Library

Make your way through the Great Gate of the Bodleian Library, directly opposite Hertford College on Catte Street.

The name 'The Bodleian Library' refers to the collection of buildings surrounding the quadrangle just inside the Great Gate. The library is the second largest in the UK: the collection comprises more than 9 million items, including some 10,000 medieval manuscripts, 1.25 million maps, 700,000 music sheets and 4 original copies of the Magna Carta all housed on over 120 miles of shelving.

Whilst the Divinity School can be visited independently (a small fee applies), the rest of the buildings are only accessible as part of a guided tour (highly recommended). Details of tours and prices can be found within the Bitesize section on page 54.

The Divinity School

The Divinity School

Walk straight ahead across the quadrangle towards the bronze statue.

The statue of The Earl of Pembroke guards the entrance to the Divinity School, the first of the buildings to be constructed on this site.

Building began on the Divinity School around 1424. It was essential that the building should be the most magnificent within the University, since it was here that the most important subject would be studied – theology. The beautiful vaulted ceiling was added after 1478 to complete the building. Funded chiefly by a donation by Thomas Kemp, Bishop of London, the ceiling was carved by a local mason, William Orchard and is a true masterpiece.

Visitors may recognise the Divinity School from the Harry Potter films, where it provides the setting for the Hogwart's Infirmary, and the home for the dancing lessons.

Duke Humfrey's Library

Duke Humfrey's Library is accessible only as part of a guided tour. If visiting independently, remain in the main quadrangle for a view of the exterior.

In 1440, Henry V's younger brother, Humphrey, Duke of Gloucester donated a large number of manuscripts to the University. In order to create space to accommodate the collection, the walls of the Divinity School were extended upwards to create a second floor. The library was finally opened in 1488, but just 60 years later in 1550, all but three books were removed following orders from Edward VI that all books referencing the Roman Catholic Church should be destroyed. With no money to replace the collection, the University decided to sell the library's furniture, and the library became a lecture room for the School of Medicine.

Entrance to Divinity School and Duke Humfrey's Library

Schools Quadrangle to The New Bodleian

Sir Thomas Bodley and the restoration of the University Library

In 1598, Sir Thomas Bodley, an English diplomat and fellow of Merton College, donated money to the University with the aim of restoring the old library.

In 1602, completely refurbished and replenished with a new collection of 2,500 books, the library re-opened. Bodley went on to forge an agreement with the Stationers Company in London whereby a copy of every book published in the country would be donated to the library. This was the forerunner of legal deposit. The Bodleian remains a legal deposit library to this day.

Schools Quadrangle

The Tower of the Five Orders

Clue 5. Find this scholarly pair. Which subjects would have been taught within their domain?

Remain in the central quadrangle.

For the remainder of his life, Bodley's fundraising efforts continued to the extent that upon his death, sufficient money remained to begin work on the Old Schools Quadrangle. The first stone of the project was laid the day after his funeral in 1613. Specifically, Bodley left money in his will for the third floor of the building which was to be used to house yet more books. The University funded the remainder of the project. To protect the books from damp, only the upper floor of the surrounding buildings was used as a library. The lower floors within the spacious quadrangle were teaching rooms where tutorials and lectures were held.

The spectacular gate-tower above the main entrance is known as the Tower of The Five Orders, referring to the five types of Classical architecture used in its design. From the bottom, they are Doric, Tuscan, Ionic, Corinthian and Composite. A statue of King James I, who was on the throne when the building was completed in 1620, looks down upon the quadrangle.

The New Bodleian

An extension to the Library, known as the New Bodleian, was built on the corner of Broad Street and Parks Road in 1937–40 to a design by Sir Giles Gilbert Scott. The project was funded partly by public subscription and partly by a large donation from the Rockefeller Foundation. A tunnel beneath Broad Street links the new and old libraries.

The New Bodleian is typical of Sir Giles Gilbert Scott's somewhat austere but functional architectural taste. His other works include Battersea Power Station and the iconic red telephone box.

The New Bodleian Library

The Radcliffe Camera to All Souls College

The Radcliffe Camera

The Radcliffe Camera

Leave Schools Quadrangle by the archway to the left of Divinity School, to Radcliffe Square.

John Radcliffe was an extremely wealthy physician in the late 17th century who, despite a fiery temper, had built a reputation as doctor to the elite. In his will he bequeathed money to the University to build a library dedicated to scientific works. It had been assumed that the library would be an extension to Schools Quadrangle, although upon reading his will, it became clear that he had a very specific location in mind for his masterpiece. A large number of shops and streets were destroyed to clear the space now known as Radcliffe Square.

The landmark shape of the Camera (meaning 'room') was inspired by Nicholas Hawksmoor, but it was architect James Gibbs' designs which were finally commissioned. Impressive as it is, the building does not lend itself well to the purpose of book storage as its curved walls are not suitable for shelving. In the early 20th century, two storeys of underground storage and a tunnel leading to the Bodleian Library were created beneath the beautifully manicured lawns. Today, the Camera remains in constant use as the main reading room for the Bodleian Library. Members of the public can visit the Camera as part of the extended Bodleian Library tour.

All Souls College

Make your way to All Souls College on the edge of Radcliffe Square.

Henry Chichele, Archbishop of Canterbury, was responsible for founding All Souls in 1438. The college was established to provide a place for advanced study, the medieval equivalent of the graduate college it remains to this day. Entry to All Souls is only available to the very highest achievers within the University. Each year, those with the top scores within the humanities subjects are invited to sit a series of additional exams to gain entry to All Souls. Only a very few are then selected, automatically becoming fellows of the college. One such fellow was T.E. Lawrence, *Lawrence of Arabia*. Despite Lawrence's lifetime of achievement, his gravestone bears the simple inscription, T.E. Lawrence, Fellow of All Souls College Oxford.

Look through the elaborate gates to the left side of the inner quadrangle. The sundial which is now displayed on the library wall was removed from the southern chapel wall, in the front quadrangle, after its restoration in 1877. Prior to its removal it was considered to be so accurate that local clock and watch makers would set their timepieces by it.

All Souls College

Clue 6. Visible from Radcliffe Square, how many angels are 'set in stone' above All Souls' stained glass chapel window?

Brasenose College to The Church of St Mary the Virgin

Brasenose College

The entrance to Brasenose College

Make your way to the opposite side of Radcliffe Square.

Brasenose College celebrated its 500th anniversary in 2009. There are many explanations given for the unusual name 'Brasenose' but the most commonly accepted is that it is linked to a nose-shaped brass, or *brazen*, door knocker belonging to the college. In the 1330s, a group of rebellious students fled from Oxford to Lincolnshire, taking with them the college door knocker. In 1890, a house in Stamford, Lincolnshire, known as Brasenose House, came on to the market. The house featured a brass, nose-shaped door knocker which college historians were convinced was that stolen from the college centuries earlier. The college purchased the house and the brass knocker was subsequently returned to its rightful home.

If open, take a moment to look around the college. The 'brazen nose' can be seen hanging above High Table within the hall and the chapel is also worth a visit. According to college legend, in 1617, the chapel provided refuge for a man named John Middleton, a giant of 9'3" in height. A portrait of the enormous man hangs above the chapel entrance, along with apparently life-sized paintings of his hands.

The Church of St Mary the Virgin

Continue to the main entrance of the church on Radcliffe Square.

Whilst also a parish church, the Church of St Mary the Virgin is commonly referred to as the University Church and many University events are held here. This association dates from around 1252 at a time when the University had no official buildings of its own and adopted the church for the purpose of official meetings, lectures and ceremonies.

Inside, look for the pillar, opposite the pulpit which has been cut to create a ledge. This is known as Cranmer's pillar. The ledge supported the structure on which Thomas Cranmer, one of the three Oxford Martyrs, was forced to stand and listen to the accusations against him on the morning he was burnt at the stake. You can read more about the Oxford Martyr's on page 41.

If you are feeling energetic, pay the admission fee and climb the 127 steps to the top of St Mary's tower. Although the steps are steep and narrow, the views from the top are wonderful and well worth the effort.

Cranmers Pillar within The Church of St Mary the Virgin

Clue 6. Not far from Cranmer's pillar, find the tribute to John Radcliffe. Which royal was among his patients?

St Mary's Lane

C. S. Lewis created Mr Tumnus based on these fawns

Make your way to High Street via St Mary's Lane.

Notice the carved figure either side of a doorway on the lane depicting two fawns. These are said to have provided C.S. Lewis with his inspiration for Mr Tumnus in the book *'The Lion, the Witch and the Wardrobe'*. The nearby lamppost is also reminiscent of the setting where Lucy first meets Tumnus upon arriving in Narnia.

Cross High Street (there is a pedestrian crossing to the left opposite The Old Bank Hotel), then make your way along Oriel Street.

Clue 7. Which former US President is commemorated on one of the brightly painted buildings on Oriel Street?

Corpus Christi College

Turn left onto Merton Street. Corpus Christi College is on the right.

Corpus Christi is the twelfth oldest college in Oxford and was founded in 1517, by the then Bishop of Winchester, Richard Foxe. Rumour has it that Foxe went blind before the completion of the college, so the students led him around the small front quad 23 times to make it seem larger than it actually is!

Originally Corpus Christi College was set to be used to house the monks from St Swythun's Priory in Winchester, but Foxe was persuaded by his contemporary and friend the Bishop of Exeter to turn its use instead to academic pursuits. Corpus Christi was therefore dedicated to the study of Classics, and remains so to this day. It still enrols more students to the faculty of Classics than any other subject.

In the main quadrangle sits a very fine example of a pillar dial. Known as the Turnbull or Pelican Sundial, this imposing focal point was erected in 1581 by Charles Turnbull. The ornate pillar is adorned with sundials, tables and verses. The Pelican Sundial can calculate the time by the sun and the moon.

The Pelican Sundial at Corpus Christi College

Merton College

Mob Quad within Merton College

Continue along Merton Street, passing a small gated lane on the right. The next college on the right is Merton.

Merton College, founded in 1264 by Walter de Merton, Lord Chancellor of England, claims to be the oldest college within the University. This claim is however disputed by both University College and Balliol College. Despite this uncertainty, Merton's 'Mob Quad' as it is known, consists of buildings dating back to the 13th and 14th centuries and is considered to be the first example of a quadrangle within the University, serving as a template for subsequent colleges. Quadrangles, featuring a central lawn surrounded on all sides by college buildings, are a well known feature of both Oxford and Cambridge Universities, although in Cambridge, they are known as 'Courts'.

The Merton Time Ceremony

This bizarre ceremony began in 1971 and takes place each year during the hour at which time is restored to Greenwich Meantime, signifying the end of British Summertime. At 1.30am, participants, all clothed in full academic dress, gather by the sundial in the Fellows' Quadrangle to drink port. At 1.50am, a toast is made to "Good Old Times", followed by a second at 1.55am "Long Live the Counter Revolution!". As the clock strikes 2am, participants begin to walk backwards around the quadrangle in an anti-clockwise direction. This continues for one hour, marking the hour that is 'lost' as the clocks are changed. The solemn procession is completed in silence.

Clue 8. On Merton Street, overlooking Merton Chapel, this former resident is noted as a Republican and a what?

Real Tennis

Continue along Merton Street, passing the Postmaster's House on the left hand side. The next large gateway on the left is the entrance to the Real Tennis Courts.

This is one just 25 remaining Real Tennis courts in England. Real Tennis takes its name from Royal Tennis and is the original racquet sport from which the modern game derives. The present court dates back to the 18th century, but records show that Real Tennis has been played here since the 16th century. The court is still in use today and the viewing gallery is open to the public on weekdays. You may even be lucky enough to catch a game in progress.

Oxford Univeristy's Real Tennis Court

University College

Unverity College

Continue along Merton Street. Parts of University College are on the left.

Although there are no records to definitively settle the argument, it is widely believed that University College is the oldest college, having been founded by William of Durham, in 1249.

A specially constructed building within the college houses a statue by Edward Onslow Ford of the poet Percy Bysshe Shelley. Despite having been expelled for his atheistic views, Shelley is now honoured as one of the college's most famous alumni. The statue has been the subject of several student pranks which have included filling the sunken area around the statue with water and live goldfish and painting the statue's private parts in bright colours!

Examination Schools

Continue along Merton Street toward High Street.

Behind the large gates on the left at the end of Merton Street are the Examination Schools. The building was constructed in 1882 as a purpose built venue for lectures and exams. The building is in constant use for lectures during term time. During summer term, tensions run high as students come here, dressed in formal black and white clothing to sit their exams. Afterwards, Merton Street also witnesses scenes of great elation as relieved students leave their final exams to begin the obligatory celebrations.

Examination Schools

The High to The Queen's College

The High

The Grand Café on 'The High'

Turn left onto High Street.

High Street, known locally simply as 'The High' was described by Nikolaus Pevsner, one of the country's leading critics on British architecture, as "one of the world's greatest streets".

The High runs from Carfax Tower to the West and Magdalen Bridge to the East. It is home to many historic University buildings and still features many specialist and independent retailers.

The Grand Café at no. 84 is a real Oxford institution. Inside, is a plaque dated 1650, which, amongst other records, leads to the claim that this is the oldest coffee house in Oxford.

Coffee houses were centres of political discussion and radical thinking and as such were closely watched by both city and university authorities. The lavish interior and tempting treats at The Grand Café make for a wonderful spot to sit and watch life on The High pass by.

Clue 9. In a fitting location next door to The Grand, search on High for a tribute to one of Oxford's famed companies. Which company?

The Queen's College

Cross High Street to The Queen's College.

The Queen's College was founded in 1341 by the chaplain of Edward III after whose wife it is named. However, the statue which looks down onto High Street is Queen Caroline who funded later improvements.

The magnificent frontage was designed by Nicholas Hawksmoor as part of a substantial rebuilding in the 18th century. The medieval foundations remain beneath the present structure.

Part of Queen's College frontage

St Edmund Hall

The Quadrangle at St Edmund Hall

Turn right into Queen's Lane and continue to St Edmund Hall on the right.

St Edmund Hall takes its name from St Edmund of Abingdon, Archbishop of Canterbury between 1234 and 1240. St Edmund's was originally a 13th century Aularian house, one of several monastic halls which provided lodging and education before the arrival of the colleges. During the 14th and 15th centuries, St Edmund's was known for its support of the teachings of reformist John Wycliffe. These were dangerous times to oppose the Roman Catholic Church and the college principal, William Taylor, was burnt at the stake as a heretic.

St Peter's at the Eastgate

Access to St Peter's at the Eastgate is via the Porter's Lodge of St Edmund Hall.

The church of St Peter at the Eastgate is hidden away in a peaceful walled enclosure surrounded by St Edmund Hall, The Queen's College and New College. The Norman parts of the church were built around 1140 by Robert D'Oilly, the then governor of Oxford.

During World War II, the crypt beneath the church was used as an air raid shelter. Since 1970, the church has been home to neighbouring St Edmund Hall's library.

St Peter's graveyard contains some interesting tombstones carved with Georgian lettering. Look for the final resting place of Sarah Hounslow, on the right of the path leading towards the church. The stone intriguingly marks the date of her death as 31st February 1835!

St Peter's at the Eastgate

Clue 10. Whether inside or outside the churchyard, this contemplative man is plain to see. Who is he?

Queen's Lane

Gargoyle on Queen's Lane

Continue along Queen's Lane.

This picturesque lane has changed little throughout the centuries and is often used in film productions such as Brideshead Revisited. The Lane is largely surrounded by high walls with few windows but some good examples of gargoyles which are a common feature of Oxford architecture can be spotted here.

New College to New College Lane

New College

The grounds of New Hall

Continue along Queen's Lane and pass beneath the stone arch to meet New College Lane. The summer entrance to New College is on the right. NB. From October to Easter, access to the college is via Holywell Street.

Despite its name, New College is actually one of the oldest colleges within the University and was founded in 1379. The college shares its official name, The College of St Mary, with Oriel College. To avoid confusion, the College became known as The New College of St Mary, shortened to New College, as it is the 'younger' of the two establishments by 55 years.

New College was founded in conjunction with Winchester College by William of Wykeham, Bishop of Winchester. Winchester was designed as a feeder to New College and both institutions focused on the education of priests, to address the shortage of clergy caused by the Black Death.

William of Wykeham is also responsible for coining the well-known phrase *"Manners Maketh Man"* which is the motto of both Winchester and New College. The motto was revolutionary for its time as it was written in English, rather than Latin.

The grounds of New College are particularly pretty and the cloisters and chapel are well worth a visit. Within the grounds you will find one of the few remaining parts of the ancient city wall which dates back to 1226. New College is responsible for the preservation of the wall and every three years an inspection is carried out by the Mayor of Oxford, a ceremony which is followed by a lavish banquet.

A Star Gazer in Residence

Continue along New College Lane until you reach the row of houses on the right, just after the lanes bears left.

No. 7 New College Lane was once the home of Edmund Halley and bears a plaque to commemorate this. Halley first came to Oxford in 1673, leaving three years later to travel to the South Atlantic island of St Helena with the intention of mapping the stars of the Southern Hemisphere. He eventually returned to Oxford as The Savilian Professor of Geometry in 1703 and took up residence here, building an observatory on his roof which is still visible today. Edmund Halley is remembered best for his work in calculating the path of the comet now named after him. He correctly predicted the date of its return but died sixteen years before its reappearance in 1742.

Edmund Halley's residence

The Pre-Raphaelites' Muse

Before passing beneath Hertford Bridge (The Bridge of Sighs), turn right along St Helen's Passage.

This narrow lane, formerly known as Hell Passage, was once one of the poorest areas of Oxford and packed full of slum dwellings. It was here in 1839, that Jane Burden was born into extreme poverty (notice the blue plaque on the wall). The daughter of a stable-hand and domestic servant, Jane had a meteoric rise to fame following a chance meeting with artists Dante Gabriel Rossetti and Edward Burne-Jones who persuaded her to model for them. Soon after, Jane modelled for William Morris, the famous Pre-Raphaelite painter and arts and crafts movement artist. The pair fell in love and married in 1859. Jane used her new position to further her education and quickly became proficient in French and Latin and a very accomplished pianist. She died in 1914, but her image lives on in galleries throughout the world.

The Turf Tavern

Continue along St Helen's Passage to the courtyard of The Turf Tavern.

The Turf Tavern is believed to be the oldest pub in Oxford and nestles beside the ancient city wall which can still be seen here.

Originally known as The Spotted Cow, the pub changed its name in the 19th century to shake off the reputation it had earned as a den of iniquity, hosting illicit gambling and cock fighting.

The images of the great and good that have enjoyed a pint or two here in recent years are displayed around the courtyard walls.

The Turf Tavern Courtyard

Clue 11. **Who went to great lengths for the Guinness at The Turf?**

Bath Place

Bath Place

Continue through the grounds of the Turf Tavern to emerge on Bath Place.

The Bath Place Hotel now occupies the 17th century cottages constructed by a group of Flemish weavers who were granted permission to build against the city wall. It is believed that the name Bath Place relates to an ancient communal well and bath house which were located here.

Congratulations you have finished Trail 1: The Heart of the University.

If you have time for more sightseeing, continue with Trail 2: Where Town Meets Gown. Don't forget to visit **www.livethecity.com** to play our free online quiz and check your clue answers. Remember, all participants will be entered into our prize draw!

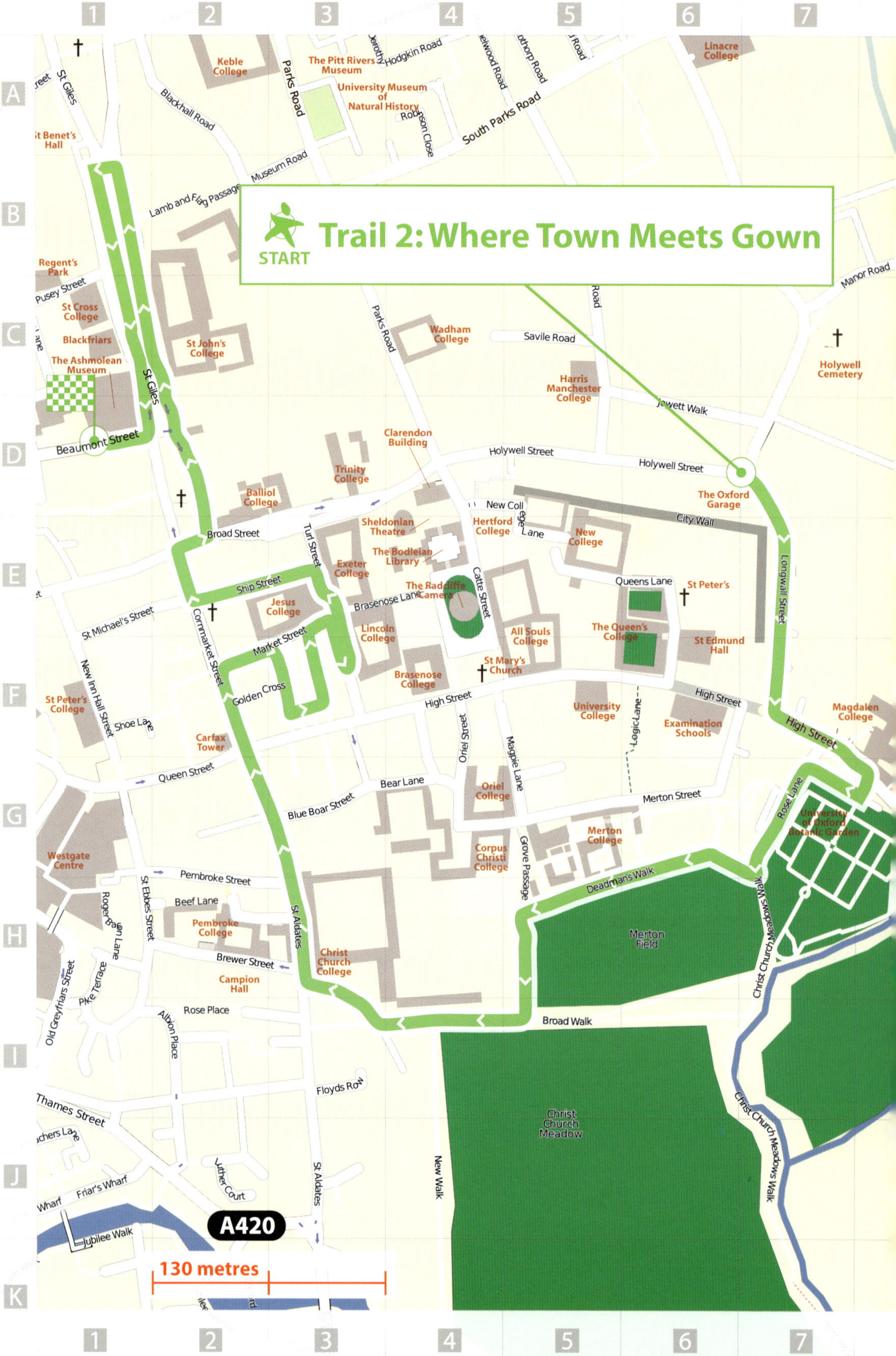
START
Trail 2: Where Town Meets Gown
Keble College
The Pitt Rivers Museum
University Museum of Natural History
Linacre College
St Giles
Parks Road
Dorothy Hodgkin Road
Blackhall Road
Robinson Close
South Parks Road
St Benet's Hall
Museum Road
Lamb and Flag Passage
Regent's Park
Pusey Street
St Cross College
Blackfriars
The Ashmolean Museum
St John's College
Wadham College
Savile Road
Manor Road
Holywell Cemetery
Harris Manchester College
Jowett Walk
Beaumont Street
Clarendon Building
Holywell Street
Trinity College
Balliol College
The Oxford Garage
New College Lane
Broad Street
Turl Street
Sheldonian Theatre
Hertford College
City Wall
New College
The Bodleian Library
Exeter College
Ship Street
The Radcliffe Camera
Catte Street
Queens Lane
St Peter's
Longwall Street
Jesus College
Brasenose Lane
St Michael's Street
Cornmarket Street
Market Street
Lincoln College
All Souls College
The Queen's College
St Edmund Hall
St Mary's Church
Golden Cross
Brasenose College
High Street
St Peter's College
New Inn Hall Street
Shoe Lane
University College
Logic Lane
Examination Schools
Magdalen College
Carfax Tower
Oriel Street
Magpie Lane
Queen Street
Bear Lane
Oriel College
Blue Boar Street
Merton Street
Rose Lane
University of Oxford Botanic Garden
Westgate Centre
Corpus Christi College
Grove Passage
Merton College
Pembroke Street
Deadman's Walk
St Ebbes Street
Beef Lane
Pembroke College
St Aldates
Merton Field
Christ Church Meadow Walk
Brewer Street
Christ Church College
Campion Hall
Old Greyfriars Street
Pike Terrace
Rose Place
Albion Place
Broad Walk
Floyds Row
Thames Street
Christ Church Meadow
New Walk
Luther Court
Friar's Wharf
Wharf
Jubilee Walk
A420
130 metres
1 2 3 4 5 6 7
A B C D E F G H I J K

Trail 2
Where Town Meets Gown

This trail is a perfect blend of 'town and gown'. Stroll through the tranquil riverside grounds of Magdalen College and neighbouring Botanic Garden. Explore the world of Christ Church College which inspired Alice's Wonderland. Learn tales of the tragic Oxford Martyrs and of the ferocious town vs gown riots.

Start: The Oxford Garage, corner of Holywell Street and Longwall Street.

Finish: The Ashmolean Museum, Beaumont Street.

Highlights:

- Christ Church College
- Botanic Garden
- The Ashmolean Museum
- Magdalen College
- The Covered Market
- The Eagle and Child Pub

Trail Time: allow around 2 hours

Distance: approximately 2 miles

No. of Clues: 10

Let's get started…

The Oxford Garage to Magdalen College

The Oxford Garage

The Oxford Garage

Clue 1. According to the photo, whose spirits were on sale at The Oxford Garage?

Begin at the corner of Holywell Street and Longwall Street.

On the right, at the corner of these two streets, is the site of the garage where William Morris famously built the first 'bullnose' Morris Oxford car in 1912. From humble beginnings in a bicycle repair shop, Morris' astounding achievements bought wealth and industry to a city which had previously been known only for its University. Known as 'The English Henry Ford', by 1914, Morris was selling around 100 cars per year, each one at a cost of £175.00.

As his empire grew, Morris became a tremendous benefactor to the city, donating enormous sums of money to found hospitals and Nuffield College which was named in his honour after he became Lord Nuffield in 1938.

Magdalen College

Continue to the end of Longwall Street. Turn left onto High Street and continue approximately 100 metres to the gates of Magdalen College.

Magdalen (pronounced Maudlin) College was founded in 1458 by William Waynefleet on the site of the former Hospital of St John. The building of the college was severely hampered by political upheaval and work did not actually commence until 1467. The wall surrounding the college grounds, known as Longwall (as the street name), was constructed first. Next came the Library, Hall and Chapel which formed the Cloister Quadrangle.

The 144ft high bell tower was completed in 1509. During the English Civil War the tower came in useful as a lookout for King Charles I's Royalist soldiers who were based in the city.

Magdalen College

Since the mid 17th century, every year at 6am on 1st May, the choristers from nearby Magdalen College School climb to the top of the tower and sing the Hymnus Eucharisticus to welcome the sun. Crowds of thousands gather at the bottom of the tower to witness the spectacle which is then followed by a day of festivities throughout the city including traditional activities such as Morris Dancing.

The grounds of Magdalen College are well worth a visit (entrance fee applies). Of particular note is the lovely chapel which contains a 15th century copy of The Last Supper by Giampetrino and beautiful stained glass windows in sepia tones. As you explore, you may well encounter the college's herd of deer which have grazed here since1705.

Penicillin Memorial

The Penicillin Memorial

Cross High Street and make your way down the steps leading towards the main entrance of the Botanic Garden.

On the right, just through the gate is the small stone Penicillin Memorial and rose garden. Whilst Alexander Fleming is most commonly associated with the discovery of penicillin, it was the team of Oxford scientists noted here who succeeded in determining its use in medicine.

Clue 2. Near the arched entrance to the Botanic Garden, find a small plaque which tells of the site's former use. When did it cease to be used for this purpose?

The Botanic Garden

If you wish to visit the Botanic Garden, make your way through the stone archway to the ticket office.

The University of Oxford Botanic Garden was founded in 1621 and is the oldest 'physic garden' in Great Britain. The garden was established after a donation of £5,000 (£3.5 million in today's money) was made by Sir Henry Danvers to create a garden for the "furtherance of learning". Despite the substantial budget, the project to build the surrounding walls and their picturesque arches, completed in 1633, left the Garden penniless.

The Botanic Garden

In 1642, the Garden was finally able to employ its first curator, Jacob Bobart, although, due to the severe shortage of funds, he was not paid for the first seven years. Bobart's skill and passion were fundamental in forming the basis of much of the Garden as it is today and an ancient English yew tree which he planted in 1645 still stands within the grounds.

Jacob Bobart was succeeded by his son who also held the position of Professor of Botany at the University, although records suggest that his shabby appearance often had him mistaken for the gardener. Bobart the Younger was responsible for introducing the process of exchanging seed samples with other gardens throughout the country, a practice which remains a very important part of the Garden's work.

Dead Man's Walk to The River Isis

Dead Man's Walk

England's first aeronaut remembered on Dead Man's Walk

Leave the Botanic Garden, continue to the end of Rose Lane and walk through the iron gates. Once through the gates, turn right and follow the path along the old city wall.

Please note that this gate is not passable for those in wheelchairs. The alternative entrance to Christ Church grounds is via St Aldates.

This path is known as Dead Man's Walk, so called as this was the funeral route once taken between the synagogue and Jewish Cemetery (now the Botanic Garden).

Look out for the plaque fixed to the city wall near the beginning of the path, which commemorates the achievements of James Sadler. On 4th October 1784, Sadler became the first Englishman to fly in a hot air balloon. In a vessel made of silk and paper with an open fire beneath, Sadler took off from Christ Church Meadow, rose to a height of almost 3,600 ft and travelled some 4 miles to land in nearby Woodeaton. Sadler repeated this incredible achievement many times during his long lifetime and despite several narrow misses, died peacefully of old age in 1828.

Christ Church Meadow

Continue along Deadman's walk and turn left to follow the path along Merton Field. The fields ahead are known as Christ Church Meadow.

This large area of pasture is owned and managed by Christ Church and borders the rivers Cherwell and Isis. During much of the year, a herd of Longhorn cattle is kept here.

This area is a popular spot with students, locals and visitors who flock here in summer months to while away the hours amidst peaceful surroundings.

Christ Church Meadow

The River Isis

The River Isis

Beyond Christ Church Meadow is the River Isis. For an optional detour follow the path opposite Christ Church to the riverside, before returning to visit the college.

Historically, the River Isis flowed all the way to Dorchester-Upon-Thames until it met The Thame to become the Thame-Isis, now abbreviated to The Thames. Since the early 20th century, only the part of the river within the boundaries of Oxford is known as the River Isis.

To the right, the large stone bridge is known as Folly Bridge. From here, pleasure boat trips along the surrounding water ways are available.

Christ Church

Christ Church

Return to the visitor's entrance of Christ Church. A tour of the college grounds is highly recommended.

Christ Church was founded on the site of the former St Frideswide's Priory in 1524 as Cardinal's College by Cardinal Wolsey, Henry VIII's Lord Chancellor. Four years later, when Henry sought to end his marriage with Katherine of Aragon to marry Anne Boleyn, Wolsey fell from grace as he was unable to persuade the Pope to agree to the annulment as quickly as the king desired.

In 1546, Henry re-named the college Christ Church. Christ Church is considered the most aristocratic college within the University and has 13 British Prime Ministers among its alumni.

A Cathedral for All

When he re-founded the college, Henry declared that its chapel would also serve as the city's cathedral. Due to this dual function, the Dean of Christ Church is always a clergyman.

Christ Church Cathedral

The Cathedral stands on the site of the 12th century priory church which was built as a shrine to house the remains of St Frideswide. Although some of the original structure was destroyed in Wolsey's efforts to build his college, thankfully, large parts remain. During Henry VIII's Dissolution of the Monasteries, the saint's shrine itself was destroyed. Some 350 years later, the fragments of the shrine were painstakingly pieced together and it now stands in the Latin Chapel in the north east corner of the Cathedral.

The Cathedral is famed for its many beautiful stained glass windows which provide an awe-inspiring backdrop for the world famous Christ Church Choir which sing here daily.

Tom Quad and Old Tom

Tom Quad

If you are not visiting the college grounds, Tom Quad is best seen via the entrance on St Aldates which we will pass shortly.

During the English Civil War, Charles I took refuge at Christ Church and conducted Parliament from the Great Hall. At the end of the war, as a mark of his gratitude, Charles awarded the college sufficient money to complete the main quadrangle, known as Tom Quad.

The quadrangle takes its name from the magnificent bell tower, Tom Tower, designed in 1682 by Sir Christopher Wren which houses Old Tom, a seven tonne bell.

Old Tom tolls 101 times every night, each toll representing one of the original 101 students of the college. The first toll sounds at 21.05, which is known as 'Oxford Time', a legacy of the days before time was standardised and Oxford was 5 minutes and 2 seconds behind Greenwich Meantime.

Christ Church to Alice's Shop

Christ Church on Camera

Christ Church Dining Hall

Christ Church has recently been featured in several film adaptations including Philip Pullman's Northern Lights and the Harry Potter series.

Many of the staircases and cloisters may be familiar, as will the Dining Hall. The film-makers for the Harry Potter series were unable to use the actual hall since it is too narrow to accommodate the four houses of the fictional Hogwarts School. Instead, an exact replica of the Dining Hall was created to a slightly larger scale – now that's magic!

Alice in Wonderland

Famously, Christ Church and its inhabitants were the inspiration behind Lewis Carroll's *Alice in Wonderland*. Alice Liddell was the daughter of the Dean of Christ Church when Charles Ludwidge Dodgson (more famously known by his pen name, Lewis Carroll) was employed at the college as the mathematics tutor.

Dodgson befriended Alice and her sisters and would take them on trips in the Oxfordshire countryside, amusing them with wonderful fairytales. With Alice as the protagonist of the stories, the other characters and settings were inspired by the people and places of Carroll's Oxford.

Illustration from Lewis Carroll's original book

Alice's Shop

Alices Shop

Leave the grounds of Christ Church via the gate leading to St Aldates.

Clue 3. Which words guide you in a journey of faith at Christ Church's threshold?

Opposite the gates of Christ Church stands a small shop, now known as Alice's Shop which was once a favourite of Alice Liddell and her sisters. The girls would go there to buy sweets before embarking on their trips with Carroll.

In *Alice's Adventures Through The Looking Glass*, the shop features as The Old Sheep Shop where the fictional Alice is surprised to find a sheep sitting behind the counter. Supposedly, the real shopkeeper had been an elderly lady with a rather bleating voice! Today, the shop is ideal for those seeking a piece of *Alice in Wonderland* memorabilia.

St Aldates

University Entrance to Christ Church

Continue along St Aldates towards the city centre passing the University entrance to Christ Church's Tom Quad on the right.

St Aldates runs from Folly Bridge to the south of the city, to Carfax Tower to the north. The street is believed to take its name from the little known Saint Aldate, although it is also possible that the name derives from the 'old gate' at the southern city wall.

The University entrance to Christ Church is via Tom Gate. For details of Evensong Services at the Cathedral, see the information board located just inside the gate.

The Museum of Oxford

Continue to the corner of Blue Boar Street.

Housed within the former Oxford Public Library, this interesting museum serves to redress the 'town/gown' balance and focuses on the non-University related history of Oxford.

Clue 4. **Who tied the knot on 6th July 1893?**

The Museum of Oxford

Town vs Gown

Continue to the corner of St Aldates and Queen Street.

An inn called the Swindlestock Tavern once stood on this site. This was the site of the infamous St Scholastica Day Riot of 1355. Members of the University enjoyed relatively privileged lifestyles compared to their fellow Oxford residents, causing great tension between 'town and gown'. Skirmishes and fights would regularly break out between the rival factions. On the night of 10th February 1355, what began as a heated exchange between a group of scholars and two townsmen quickly escalated into a full scale battle. When the fighting eventually ceased, 63 scholars and 30 townsfolk were dead. Due to its powerful connections, the University was absolved of blame and granted yet more power over the city. As penance for the crimes of the 'town', it was decreed that the Mayor of Oxford should pay one penny each year to the University. The Mayor's Oath as it became known continued until 1859, when the incoming Mayor refused to uphold the tradition.

Clue 5. **We'll bank on you to discover how long the Swindlestock Tavern was in business.**

Carfax Tower

Carfax Tower with St Martin and the beggar

Cross Queen Street.

Carfax Tower is considered to be at the absolute centre of the city and the name Carfax derives from the French 'carrefour' or 'crossroads'. Today, the tower is all that remains of the 13th century St Martin's Church. The church's namesake, St Martin, is the patron saint of beggars. The stone engraving above the archway to the right of the tower depicts the famous story associated with him. Legend has it that upon seeing a poorly clothed beggar passing by, Martin cut his own cloak in two and gave one half to the poor man. When he awoke the next morning, the cloak had miraculously been restored.

St Martin's was the official city church and as such was historically where the mayor and other officials would worship. In 1896, the main body of the church was demolished to widen the surrounding streets and All Saints Church on High Street became the new city church.

The Covered Market

Walk along Cornmarket Street, turning right in Market Street. The Covered Market is halfway along the street on the right hand side.

The present day indoor market has its origins in the street markets of Oxford, records of which date back to the 13th century, although it is strongly believed that markets were held as long ago as the 9th century.

Markets were often dirty and chaotic and so in the 18th century, a covered market was proposed and established in order to clean up Oxford's streets. The present day market retains the high roofs built in the 19th century.

Today's market is full of independent shops and refreshment venues with something to interest everyone. In particular, look out for the fabulous cake shop where amazing masterpieces are created in full view of passersby.

The Covered Market

Clue 6. Find the timely 'Gent's' within the Covered Market, not far from the Golden Cross. Where do they come from?

Turl Street

Turl Street

Return to Market Street and continue to Turl Street.

In the 14th century Turl Street was known as St Mildred's Street and ended at a gate in the city wall. In the 17th century it became Turlgate Street apparently having acquired the name due to the twirling gate which was in the city wall. The name has since been shortened to Turl Street.

Lincoln College

To the right of Brasenose Lane is Lincoln College.

Lincoln College is one of the smallest Oxford colleges. The 15th century facade of its medieval hall and the 17th century chapel are its most attractive and important buildings.

Founded in 1427 by the then Bishop of Lincoln, hence its name, the college had close links with Lincolnshire, Nottinghamshire and Yorkshire and originally, many of its students came from these areas.

Student numbers rose significantly during the 17th century, with many 'gentlemen commoners' joining the college. In return for extra privileges, these wealthy individuals were required to donate a piece of silver, many of which can still be found in the college collection. One of Lincoln's most famous students was John Wesley, founder of the Methodist movement.

Lincoln College and John Welsey

Clue 7. **How many silver geese fly at the feet of St Mildred at Lincoln's entrance?**

Jesus College

Sculpture at Jesus College

Jesus College stands at the corner of Market Street and Turl Street.

Jesus College, founded in 1571, is the only college in Oxford to date from the reign of Queen Elizabeth I and was established to educate future clergymen. The college founder was Hugh Aprice, a churchman from the Welsh town of Brecon. Due to this association, the college became known as 'the Welsh college' retaining strong links with Wales. Indeed, between 1571 and 1915 Jesus had only one non-Welsh principal.

Although in later years the college began to welcome students of other nationalities, until the 19th century it was essential for all students to have some knowledge of the Welsh language.

Exeter College to St Michael at the Northgate

Exeter College

Exeter College Chapel

Cross to the opposite side of Turl Street to Exeter College.

Exeter College was founded in 1314 by Bishop Walter de Stapeldon of Exeter to establish a means of educating the clergy in his diocese.

If open, the college chapel is well worth a visit. Modelled in part on the Sainte Chappelle in Paris, this beautiful building contains many works by the Pre-Raphaelite artists Edward Burne Jones and William Morris who both attended the college. A bronze bust of former Exeter student J. R. R. Tolkien can be found within the ante-chapel.

Other notable alumni from the fields of art and literature include playwright Alan Bennett and authors Martin Amis and Philip Pullman. Fans of Colin Dexter's *Morse* series will recognise the Quadrangle as the spot where the inspector died.

St Michael at the Northgate

From Turl Street, turn left into Ship Street and walk to the junction with Cornmarket Street. St Michael at the Northgate is on the right hand side.

Dating back to before the Norman Conquest of 1066, the tower of St Michael's is the oldest building within the city. Originally, the structure would have stood at the Northern entrance to the city walls, hence its full name.

For a small fee, visitors can climb the Saxon tower. At the bottom of the stairs, look out for the records which tell of the untimely end of one poor chap who died after falling from the top of the tower. At first floor level is The Treasury which houses a collection of rare silverware belonging to the church. Here too is a copy of the marriage certificate of artist William Morris and Jane Burden who were married in the church in 1859. Continuing up the tower is the original door from the Martyrs' prison cell.

For centuries, the foreboding Bocado Prison stood beside St Michael's Church. It was here that the Oxford Martyrs (Hugh Latimer, Nicholas Ridley and Thomas Cranmer) were incarcerated before their eventual executions.

The tower of St Michael at the Northgate

Clue 8. Which saint can be found on St Michael's Street?

The Martyrs' Cross

The Martyrs' Cross

From Cornmarket Street, continue to Broad Street. Make your way through the traffic barrier in the middle of the street and walk approximately 50 metres straight ahead.

In the 16th century, St Michael's church and the Bocardo Prison were at the Northern extremity of the city. Beyond this, what is now Broad Street was then nothing more than a ditch outside the city wall. It was in this spot that the Oxford Martyrs' were burnt at the stake in 1555 and 1556. Cranmer is said to have watched Latimer and Ridley's execution from his cell.

The Oxford Martyrs'

When Mary I (otherwise known as Bloody Mary) came to the throne in 1553, she set out to quash the Protestant faith and return England to Roman Catholicism, arresting and executing anyone opposed to her views. The Oxford Martyrs', Hugh Latimer, Nicholas Ridley and Thomas Cranmer were all vocal supporters of the Protestant faith.

Latimer and Ridley were the first to be tried and burnt at the stake here in Oxford on 16th October 1555. Latimer's famous last words at the stake were: "Be of good cheer, Master Ridley, and play the man, for we shall this day light such a candle in England as I trust by God's grace shall never be put out."

After a long struggle with his conscience, Cranmer initially wrote a letter of submission to the Pope, stating his acceptance of the Catholic faith. Despite this, Queen Mary refused to believe that the submission was sincere and ordered Cranmer to be burnt in Oxford on 21st March 1556. At the last moment, in an act of defiance, Cranmer withdrew his submission and re-affirmed his Protestant faith. In a passionate speech he declared "i have sinned, in that I signed with my hand what I did not believe with my heart. When the flames are lit, this hand shall be the first to burn". Indeed, when the fire was lit, he leant forward and unflinchingly held his right hand in the flames.

The Martyrs' Memorial

Retrace your steps along Broad Street and turn right into Magdalene Street East. Continue to the fork in the road.

As well as serving as a monument to the Martyrs, when it was built, the memorial was seen by some as a strong political statement against the 19th century Oxford Movement.

The Oxford Movement was lead by John Keble and John Henry Newman along with other prominent members of the University community. Broadly speaking it was concerned with promoting a Catholic revival in the Church of England. This very pro-Protestant memorial was seen by many as a mark of defiance against the movement.

The Martyrs' Memorial

St John's College to The Eagle and Child Pub

St John's College

St John's College

Continue along the right hand side of St Giles.

St John's College was founded by wealthy cloth merchant and Lord Mayor of London, Sir Thomas White in 1555. White was a staunch supporter of the Counter Reformation of Queen Mary I (Bloody Mary) and established the college to educate Catholic clergymen.

In later centuries St John's gained a reputation for excellence in medicine and law. Among the many notable St John's alumni are the 17th century agriculturalist Jethro Tull, poet Philip Larkin and former British Prime Minister, Tony Blair.

St John's is believed to be the wealthiest college within the University, owning much of the land in Oxford and beyond. The college grounds are beautiful and well worth exploring.

St Giles Fair

Continue along St Giles, crossing at the pedestrian crossing to St Giles Church.

The 13th century church of St Giles stands between Woodstock and Banbury Road. This area is the location of the annual St Giles Fair, an ancient tradition which dates back to 1624.

What began life as a religious occasion to celebrate the life of St Giles, by Victorian times, had transformed into a rowdy spectacle complete with fairground attractions and a freak show. The fair is still held each September, thankfully minus the freak show, but still with its fair share of carousels and candy floss.

Clue 9. **On the green, find the worldly time-piece to discover which city Oxford is twinned with.**

The Eagle and Child Pub

The Eagle and Child pub

Walk along the right hand side of St Giles back towards the city centre.

This 17th century pub was sold by University College to nearby St John's College in 2003. The pub is most famous as the meeting place for the literary group, The Inklings, whose members included C. S. Lewis and J. R. R. Tolkein.

Clue 10. **Do you have the smallest idea when the literary group's meetings took place?**

The Randolph Hotel to The Ashmolean Museum

The Randolph Hotel

The Randolph Hotel

Continue along St Giles and turn right into Beaumont Street. The impressive building ove the road is the Randolph Hotel.

The Randolph is a prestigious five star establishment built in 1864.

A favourite of dignitaries and famous names for almost 150 years, the hotel was also the preferred watering hole of the Oxford based Inspector Morse. The Morse bar within the hotel is a lasting tribute to the world famous sleuth.

The Ashmolean Museum

Continue on Beaumont Street to the entrance to The Ashmolean is on the right.

This grand and imposing structure was built in 1845 as the new home for the collections formerly housed in the Old Ashmolean on Broad Street. The museum re-opened in late 2009 following a £61 million refurbishment to designs by world-famous architect Rick Mather.

The gallery space has been doubled, enabling thousands of objects previously kept in storage to be put on display for all to enjoy. The museum hosts a regular programme of events which encourage interactive discovery visitors of all ages.

Inside visitors can explore fascinating collections of art and antiquities which span the centuries and the globe. The Museum's greatest treasure is The Alfred Jewel, believed to have belonged to King Alfred the Great (871–899AD). Look out too for the robes once worn by Lawrence of Arabia.

Another new addition to the museum is the rooftop restaurant, the first of its kind in the city, where visitors can relax over lunch or afternoon tea whilst enjoying views across the Oxford skyline.

The Main Staircase and the new Atrium of the Ashmolean Museum

Congratulations! You have finished Trail 2: Where Town Meets Gown. Don't forget to visit **www.livethecity.com** to play our free online quiz and check your clue answers. Remember, all participants will be entered into our prize draw!

GORING

Oxford University is the oldest university within the English speaking world. Although the exact date of foundation is unknown, it is clear that the city was home to a number of educational establishments from as early as the 11th century.

In 1209, following violent fighting between University scholars and townsmen, a group of students fled the city, eventually arriving in Cambridge to form the university there. Fierce rivalry still exists between these two establishments, each referring to the other as 'The Other Place'.

Today, the University consists of 38 colleges and 6 Permanent Private Halls (smaller educational establishments which normally offer only religious teaching). The University is governed by a central administration which is headed by the Vice Chancellor.

Competition for a place at Oxford is extremely fierce. Applicants today must display excellent communication skills at interview, the necessary drive and determination to succeed along with the essential top grade A Level results. In recent years, the University has greatly improved its intake policy, with around 50% of all undergraduates now coming from state schools.

When applying to Oxford, students apply to the University rather than to a college, although they may specify a preference. The colleges provide for the welfare of the students and lectures are conducted within the relevant University departments. There is of course intense rivalry between members of the various colleges, none more prevalent than between the numerous sporting teams.

An A–Z isting of all the Oxford Colleges

With the exception of exam periods, many of the colleges are open to visitors after 2pm. To help you select the ones you'd like to visit, we have compiled a list of all the Oxford colleges including location, contact details and admission charges where applicable.

1. All Souls College founded 1438

INFO: Each of All Souls' members automatically become Fellows, a system unique to Oxford.
SIZE: 76 fellows, 24 emeritus.
ALUMNI: Marchmont Nedham ("press agent" to Oliver Cromwell), Sir Edward Seymour (Speaker of the House of Commons 1679).
ADDRESS: High Street, OX1 4AL. Tel: 01865 279379.
VISITING: Free, check with Porter's Lodge before visiting.

2. Balliol College founded 1263–8

INFO: Although no records exist to confirm a precise construction date, Balliol is one of the oldest Oxford colleges.
SIZE: 378 undergraduates, 332 graduates.
ALUMNI: John Wycliffe (translated the Bible into English).
ADDRESS: Broad Street, OX1 3BJ. Tel: 01865 277777.
VISITING: £2 (students 50p, children free).

3. Brasenose College — founded 1509

INFO: Origins of this College's unusual name are unknown, although one theory is that it comes from a brazen (bronze) door knocker.
SIZE: 346 undergraduates, 200 graduates.
ALUMNI: John Buchan (writer and statesman), Robert Runcie (Archbishop of Canterbury), Colin Cowdrey (Cricketer).
ADDRESS: Radciffe Square, OX1 4AJ. Tel: 01865 277830.
VISITING: £1.50 when open.

4. Christ Church — founded 1546

INFO: One of the largest colleges and the cathedral chuch for the diocese of Oxford.
SIZE: 392 undergraduates, 200 graduates.
ALUMNI: David Dimbleby (broadcaster), Robert Peel (Prime Minister and founder of the Metropolitan Police Force), Lewis Carroll (author).
ADDRESS: St Aldate's, OX1 1DP. Tel: 01865 276150.
VISITING: £6 (£4.50 concs, £12 family).

5. Corpus Christi College — founded 1517

INFO: Catherine of Aragon visited here while Henry VIII hunted at Woodstock.
SIZE: 231 undergraduates, 115 graduates.
ALUMNI: Thomas Arnold (educational reformer), Vikram Seth (writer), David Miliband (politician).
ADDRESS: Merton Street, OX1 4JF. Tel: 01865 276700.
VISITING: Free, check with Porter's Lodge before visiting.

6. Exeter College — founded 1314

INFO: The fictitious television character *Inspector Morse* died in Exeter Front Quad.
SIZE: 320 undergraduates, 200 graduates.
ALUMNI: J.R. Tolkien (writer), Edward Burne Jones (artist), Philip Pullman (writer).
ADDRESS: Turl Street, OX1 3DP. Tel: 01865 279600.
VISITING: Free, check with Porter's Lodge before visiting.

7. Green Templeton College — founded 2008

INFO: Newest college formed by merger of Green College and Templeton College, based at the Radcliffe Observatory site.
SIZE: 500 graduates.
ALUMNI: James Lovelock (scientist), Sir Richard Dole (doctor and lung cancer/tobacco research).
ADDRESS: Woodstock Road, OX2 6HG. Tel: 01865 274770.
VISITING: Normally closed to visitors.

8. Harris Manchester College — founded 1889

INFO: Solely dedicated to mature students. The Chapel has a Burne Jones stained glass window.
SIZE: 73 undergraduates, 112 graduates.
ALUMNI: Walter Jenkins Evans (welsh academic), Sir Oliver Popplewell (judge), Joe Roff (Australian rugby player).
ADDRESS: Mansfield Road, OX1 3TD. Tel: 01865 271006.
VISITING: Free, check with Porter's Lodge before visiting.

9. Hertford College — founded 1740

INFO: Home of the famous Bridge of Sighs, known more correctly as Hertford Bridge.
SIZE: 365 undergraduates, 220 graduates.
ALUMNI: William Tyndale (protestant martyr), Jonathon Swift (writer and political commentator), Evelyn Waugh (writer).
ADDRESS: Catte Street, OX1 3BW. Tel: 01865 279400.
VISITING: Normally closed to visitors.

10. Jesus College — founded 1571

INFO: Founded by Elizabeth I, this College has had Welsh connections throughout history.
SIZE: 325 undergraduates, 150 graduates.
ALUMNI: T. E. Lawrence (of Arabia), Norman Manley (Jamaican Prime Minister), Harold Wilson (Prime Minister).
ADDRESS: Turl Street, OX1 3DW. Tel: 01865 279700.
VISITING: Free, check with Porter's Lodge before visiting.

11. Keble College — founded 1870

INFO: Benefactor William Gibbs' fortune was founded on Peruvian bird droppings, a valuable fertiliser!
SIZE: 396 undergraduates, 222 graduates.
ALUMNI: Imran Khan (Pakistani cricketer and politician), Chad Varah (founder of the Samaritans).
ADDRESS: Parks Road, OX1 3PG. Tel: 01865 272727.
VISITING: Free, check with Porter's Lodge before visiting.

12. Kellogg College — founded 1990

INFO: Unique in the Oxford system in that it accepts part time students to allow them to combine studies with other responsibilities.
SIZE: 550 full and part time students.
ALUMNI: Joseph Van Maltzahn (British rower), Kevin Tkachuk (Canadian rugby player).
ADDRESS: Banbury Road, OX2 6PN. Tel: 01865 612000.
VISITING: Free, check with Porter's Lodge before visiting.

13. Lady Margaret Hall — founded 1878

INFO: The first womens' college in Oxford.
SIZE: 377 undergraduates, 170 graduates.
ALUMNI: Antonia Fraser (writer), Nigella Lawson (celebrity chef), Ann Widdecombe (politician).
ADDRESS: Norham Gardens, OX2 6QA. Tel: 01865 274300.
VISITING: Free, check with Porter's Lodge before visiting.

14. Linacre College — founded 1962

INFO: This College's name commemorates Thomas Linacre, c. 1460–1524, one of the greatest scholars of his time.
SIZE: Approximately 300 students.
ALUMNI: Yasmin Alibhai-Brown (journalist), Stephen Venner (bishop).
ADDRESS: St Cross Road, OX1 3JA. Tel: 01865 271650.
VISITING: Normally closed to visitors.

15. Lincoln College founded 1427

INFO: One of the smallest colleges within the University, Lincoln's most famous alumnus is John Wesley, founder of the Methodist movement.
SIZE: 283 undergraduates, 299 graduates.
ALUMNI: John Le Carre (author), Eve Best (actress).
ADDRESS: Turl Street, OX1 3DR. Tel: 01865 279800.
VISITING: Free, check with Porter's Lodge before visiting.

16. Magdalen College founded 1458

INFO: Counts 9 Nobel prize winners among its alumni.
SIZE: 371 undergraduates, 264 graduates.
ALUMNI: John Betjeman (poet – left without his degree), Ian Hislop (politician), Robert Hardy (actor).
ADDRESS: High Street, OX1 4AU. Tel: 01865 276000.
VISITING: £4 (£3 concs). Check with Porter's Lodge before visiting.

17. Mansfield College founded 1886

INFO: Dr Albert Schweitzer was a special lecturer and performed on the chapel organ.
SIZE: 213 undergraduates, 80 graduates.
ALUMNI: Paul Crossley (pianist), Stephan Pollard (journalist).
ADDRESS: Mansfield Road, OX1 3TF. Tel: 01865 270999.
VISITING: Free, check with Porter's Lodge before visiting.

18. Merton College founded 1264

INFO: The library found in the Mob Quadrangle is the oldest continuously functioning library in the world.
SIZE: 291 undergraduates.
ALUMNI: Roger Bannister (ran the 4 minute mile), Kris Kristofferson (musician), William Harvey (groundbreaking physician).
ADDRESS: Merton Street, OX1 4JD. Tel: 01865 276310.
VISITING: Free, check with Porter's Lodge before visiting.

19. New College founded 1379

INFO: Famous choir perform every day at Choral service during term time (apart from on Wednesdays).
SIZE: 375 undergraduates, 180 graduates.
ALUMNI: Tony Benn (socialist politician), John Galsworthy (novelist), Joseph Horovitz (composer and conductor).
ADDRESS: Holywell Street, OX1 3BN. Tel: 01865 279555.
VISITING: Free, check with Porter's Lodge before visiting.

20. Nuffield College founded 1937

INFO: Founded by William Morris (Lord Nuffield) founder of Morris Motors Ltd.
SIZE: 75 graduates.
ALUMNI: Manmohan Singh (Indian Prime Minister), Austin Mitchell (politician), Mark J Carney (Govenor of the Bank of Canada).
ADDRESS: New Road, OX1 1NF. Tel: 01865 278500.
VISITING: Free, check with Porter's Lodge before visiting.

21. Oriel College — founded 1326

INFO: In 1948, Queen Elizabeth II (whilst Duchess of Edinburgh) was greeted in the Front Quad by the college tortoise.
SIZE: 282 undergraduates, 180 graduates.
ALUMNI: Matthew Arnold (poet), "Beau" Brummell (regency dandy), Gilbert White (naturalist).
ADDRESS: Oriel Square, OX1 4EW. Tel: 01865 276555.
VISITING: Occasionally open to visitors, please check.

22. Pembroke College — founded 1624

INFO: Samuel Johson attended for 1 year in 1728 but ran out of money. He was awarded an honourary degree in1775.
SIZE: 359 undergraduates, 115 graduates.
ALUMNI: Michael Heseltine (politician), J. William Fulbright (scholarships), Honeysuckle Weeks (actress).
ADDRESS: St Aldate's, OX1 1DW. Tel: 01865 276444.
VISITING: Normally closed to visitors.

23. The Queen's College — founded 1341

INFO: Named after Queen Phillipa of Hainault (wife of King Edward III).
SIZE: 304 undergraduates, 160 graduates.
ALUMNI: Rowan Atkinson (actor/writer), Ruth Kelly (politician), Thomas Middleton (Jacobean playwright).
ADDRESS: High Street, OX1 4AW. Tel: 01865 279120.
VISITING: Normally closed to visitors.

24. St Anne's College — founded 1879

INFO: Founded as The Society of Home Students to promote equal opportunities, with a focus on women's rights.
SIZE: 418 undergraduates, 253 graduates.
ALUMNI: Penelope Lively (novelist), Libby Purves (radio presenter, journalist and author), Maria Aitken (actress, writer and director).
ADDRESS: Woodstock Road, OX2 6HS. Tel: 01865 274800.
VISITING: Free, check with Porter's Lodge before visiting.

25. St Anthony's College — founded 1953

INFO: The first Warden of the College, Sir William Deakin, was an aide to Winston Churchill during WWII.
SIZE: 400+ graduates.
ALUMNI: John Redwood (politician), Anne Applebaum (journalist and Pulitzer prize winner).
ADDRESS: Woodstock Road, OX2 6JF. Tel: 01865 284700.
VISITING: Free, check with Porter's Lodge before visiting.

26. St Catherine's College — founded 1963

INFO: Celebrations of the College's patron saint include a giant catherine wheel being lit in the quad.
SIZE: 453 undergraduates, 246 graduates.
ALUMNI: Benazir Bhutto (Pakistani politician), Joseph Heller (author of *Catch 22*), Matthew Pinsett olympic (rower and broadcaster).
ADDRESS: Manor Road, OX1 3UJ. Tel: 01865 271700.
VISITING: Free, check with Porter's Lodge before visiting.

27. St Cross College founded 1965

INFO: A postgraduate only College, with an international intake.
SIZE: 400 graduates.
ALUMNI: Tim Foster (olympic rower), Toshiharu Furukawa (Japenese politicia), Richard Rudgley (anthroplogist).
ADDRESS: St Giles', OX1 3LZ. Tel: 01865 278490.
VISITING: Normally closed to visitors.

28. St Edmund Hall founded 1278

INFO: Buildings include the only surviving medieval academic structures.
SIZE: 373 undergraduates, 175 graduates.
ALUMNI: Sir Robin Day (broadcaster), Al Murray (comedian, Terry Jones (Monty Python team and film director).
ADDRESS: Queen's Lane, OX1 4AR. Tel: 01865 279000.
VISITING: Free, check with Porter's Lodge before visiting.

29. St Hilda's College founded 1893

INFO: Named after St Hilda of Whitby and founded to promote women's education.
SIZE: 387 undergraduates, 110 graduates.
ALUMNI: Victoria Hislop (novelist), Barbara Pym (writer), Tsuda Omeko (pioneer for education for Japanese women).
ADDRESS: Cowley Place, OX4 1DY. Tel: 01865 276884.
VISITING: Normally closed to visitors.

30. St Hugh's College founded 1886

INFO: Founded by Elizabeth Wordsworth, great niece of the famous poet.
SIZE: 394 undergraduates, 261 graduates.
ALUMNI: Aung San Suu Kyi (human rights activist), Emily Davison (suffragette), Barbara Castle (socialist politician).
ADDRESS: St Margaret's Road, OX2 6LE. Tel; 01865 274900.
VISITING: Normally closed to visitors.

31. St John's College founded 1555

INFO: Attended by Jane Austen's father and brothers.
SIZE: 370 undergraduates, 260 graduates.
ALUMNI: A. E. Housman (poet), Tony Blair (prime minister), Kingsley Amis (writer).
ADDRESS: St Giles', OX1 3JP. Tel: 01865 277300.
VISITING: Free, check with Porter's Lodge before visiting.

32. St Peter's College founded 1929

INFO: Founded by Bishop Francis James Chavasse, inspiration and prime motivation behind the building of Liverpool Cathedral.
SIZE: 324 undergraduates, 135 graduates.
ALUMNI: Rev. W. Awdry (creator of *Thomas The Tank Engine*), Ken Roach (film director), Hugh Fearnley Whittingstall (celebrity chef).
ADDRESS: New Inn Hall Street, OX1 2DL. Tel: 01865 278900.
VISITING: Free, check with Porter's Lodge before visiting.

33. Trinity College founded 1554

INFO: The Chapel was designed by Dean Aldrich with advice from Christopher Wren.
SIZE: 288 undergraduates, 119 graduates.
ALUMNI: Ross and Norris McWhirter (founders of *The Guiness Book of Records*), Sir Richard Burton (explorer), Anthony Crossland (politician).
ADDRESS: Broad Street, OX1 3BH. Tel: 01865 279900.
VISITING: £2 (£1 children). Check with Porter's Lodge before visiting.

34. Somerville College founded 1879

INFO: The inspiration behind Shrewsbury College in the novel Gaudy Night by Dorothy L. Sayers.
SIZE: 363 undergraduates, 104 graduates.
ALUMNI: Dorothy Hodgkin (Nobel Prize winner), Indira Gandhi (Indian prime minister), Margaret Thatcher (prime minister).
ADDRESS: Woodstock Road, OX2 6HD. Tel: 01865 270600.
VISITING: Free, check with Porter's Lodge before visiting.

35. University College founded 1249

INFO: Percy Bysshe Shelley, the major Romantic poet, was expelled after 1 year. Also attended by Prince Felix Yusupov, the assassin of Rasputin.
SIZE: 361 undergraduates, 150 graduates.
ALUMNI: Professor Stephen Hawking, C. S. Lewis (author), Bill Clinton (US President).
ADDRESS: High Street, OX1 4BH. Tel: 01865 276602.
VISITING: Normally closed to visitors.

36. Wadham College founded 1610

INFO: A monument in the chapel to Thomas Harris appears to be made of a stack of books.
SIZE: 416 undergraduates, 150 graduates.
ALUMNI: Melvyn Bragg (author and broadcaster), Sir Thomas Beecham (conductor and impresario), Cecil Day-Lewis (poet).
ADDRESS: Parks Road, OX1 3PN. Tel: 01865 277900.
VISITING: Free, check with Porter's Lodge before visiting.

37. Wolfson College founded 1965

INFO: Purpose built on the banks of the Cherwell – the only college with its own onsite punt harbour.
SIZE: Around 620 graduates.
ALUMNI: Karim Ahmad Khan (human rights lawyer), Henry Hardy (author).
ADDRESS: Linton Road, OX2 6UD. Tel: 01865 274100.
VISITING: Normally closed to visitors.

38. Worcester College founded 1714

INFO: Oscar Wilde said of the chapel "As a piece of simple decorative and beautiful art it is perfect".
SIZE: 388 undergraduates, 198 graduates.
ALUMNI: Richard Adams (author), Stephen Oliver (composer), Rupert Murdoch (media mogul).
ADDRESS: Walton Street, OX1 2HB. Tel: 01865 278300.
VISITING: Free, check with Porter's Lodge before visiting.

10 THINGS YOU MUST DO IN Oxford

1. Visit An Oxford College

With 38 colleges to choose from, there are plenty of opportunities to peek behind the scenes of this world famous University. Many colleges are open to visitors, with the exception of exam periods. Our list of colleges gives details of opening times and any applicable admission charges.

2. Ssssssh! Tour the Bodleian Library

Learn about The Bodleian's fascinating history and to gain access to the otherwise off-limits areas. The extended tour includes the Radcliffe Camera.

Standard Tour: (1 hour), Monday – Saturday, 10.30, 11.30, 2 and 3, £6. Short Tour (30 mins), Monday – Saturday, 4, £4. Extended Tour (1.5 hours) Saturdays at 10, £12. Sunday tours also available, enquire at the Great Gate
Telephone: 01865 277224

3. Behind Bars at Oxford Castle Unlocked

Explore the ancient remains of this former castle and prison. Costumed character guides are on-hand to reveal the site's fascinating history.
Opening Times: Open daily from 10.00 (last tour 4.20). Closed from 24th–26th December
Admission: Adults, £7.75, Children £5.50 and Conc., £6.50
Address: 44–46 Oxford Castle, Oxford OX1 1AY
Telephone: 01865 260666
Website: www.oxfordcastleunlocked.co.uk

4. Visit a Literary Pub

The pubs of Oxford have inspired many a famous author. The Eagle and Child on St Giles was frequented by 'The Inklings' including members J. R. R. Tolkein and C. S. Lewis. The Lamb and Flag, also on St Giles, provided inspiration for Thomas Hardy's *Jude The Obscure*, and The Mitre, on the corner of Turl Street and The High, was a favourite of Oscar Wilde. The White Horse on Broad Street frequently features in the *Inspector Morse* series.

5. A Bird's Eye View

Climb to the top of St Mary's Church and if the 127 steps don't take your breath away, the spectacular views surely will.

Opening Times: 9–5 year round and 9–6 in July and August
Admission: Free admission to the church, with £3 charge to climb the tower for adults and £2.50 for children
Address: Main entrance via Radcliffe Square, Oxford
Telephone: 01865 279 112
Website: www.university-church.ox.ac.uk

6. Go Punting

No trip to Oxford is complete without a punting trip. Punts are flat bottomed, wooden boats which are propelled along using a long pole pushed against the river bed. Whether you feel brave enough to try yourself or prefer the more leisurely option of a chauffeured trip, be sure to try this traditional Oxford pastime.

Magdalen Bridge Boathouse: Open daily, 10am til dusk
Telephone: 01865 202643

7. Take a Boat Trip

Escape the bustle of the city and explore the surrounding area on a boat trip along the Thames. From self drive options to private charters and sightseeing cruises, there are options to suite all budgets.

Salter's Steamers: Folly Bridge (at the bottom of St Aldates)
Telephone: 01865 243421

8. Shopping at The Covered Market

Explore the wide range of independent retailers and boutique shops within the Covered Market. You'll find everything from fresh produce to high fashion and plenty of opportunities for window shopping as well as spending your pennies. Look out for The Cake Shop, where delicious masterpieces are created in the shop front in full view of passersby.

The Covered Market, Market Street: Open Monday to Saturday, 8–5.30; Sunday, 10–4

9. Evensong at Christ Church Cathedral

Enjoy a spiritually uplifting experience and attend one of the world famous Evensong services at Christ Church Cathedral.

Services are at 6.05pm during term time (excluding Mondays) and last for 45 minutes. For more information, check the notice-board just inside the Tom Gate on St Aldates. Services are free. Arrive at least half an hour early to avoid disappointment.

10. Addison's Walk

Within the grounds of Magdalen College, is a riverside path known as Addison's Walk. This was the site of the late night stroll taken by J. R. R. Tolkien, Hugo Dyson and C. S. Lewis, where Lewis was inspired to convert to Christianity. In April and May, a meadow beside the walk is filled with rare wild flowers called Snakeshead Frittilaries.

Access is via Magdalen College when open. An admission charge of £4 for adults and £3 for concs. and children applies.

10 MUSEUMS TO VISIT IN Oxford

The Alfred Jewel at the Ashmolean Museum

1. Oxford Museum of Natural History

Home to such far ranging exhibits as Oxford's dinosaurs, Lewis Carroll's Alice collection, and the Oxford Dodo!

Opening Times: 10–5, 7 days a week
Admission: Free
Address: Parks Road, OX1 3PW
Telephone: +44 (0)1865 272950
Website: www.oum.ox.ac.uk

2. Pitt Rivers Museum

A truly fascinating museum founded by General Pitt-Rivers, a leading figure in the archaeological and anthropological world.

Opening Times: 10–4.30 Tuesday – Sunday and Bank Holiday Mondays; 12–4.30 all other Mondays
Admission: Free
Address: Parks Road, OX1 3PP
Telephone: +44 0(1865) 270927
Website: www.prm.ox.ac.uk

3. Ashmolean Museum

Considered by many to be the most important museum of art and archaeology in the world.

Opening Times: 10–6 Tuesday – Sunday. (Closed Mondays)
Admission: Free
Address: Beaumont Street, OX1 2PH
Telephone: +44 (0)1865 278000.
Website: www.ashmolean.org

4. Museum of the History of Science

A fascinating collection of early scientific instruments in the world's oldest surviving purpose-built museum building.

Opening Times: 12.00–5.00 Tuesday – Friday; 10–5 Saturday; 2–5 Sunday. (Closed Mondays)
Admission: Free
Address: Broad Street, OX1 3AZ
Telephone: +44 (0) 1865 277280
Website: www.mhs.ox.ac.uk

5. Bate Collection of Musical Instruments

One of the most prominent collections of musical instruments in the world.

Opening Times: Mon – Fri 2–5 excl. Easter & Christmas; Sat (during term time) 10–12. (Closed Sun)
Admission: Free
Address: St Aldate's, OX1 1DB
Telephone: +44 (0)1865 276139
Website: www.bate.ox.co.uk

6. Christ Church Picture Gallery

Regarded as one of the most important private collections of Old Master drawings in the country.

Opening Times: May – end Sep: Mon – Sat, 10.30–5, Sun 2–5. October – end Apr: Mon – Sat10.30–1, Sun, 2–4.30
Admission: Adults £3.00 Concessions £2
Address: St Aldate's, OX1 1DP
Telephone: +44 (0)1865 276172
Website: www.chch.ox.ac.uk

7. Modern Art Museum

This is the largest museum devoted to modern art in the South of England.

Opening Times: Tuesday – Saturday 10–5, Sunday 12–5. (Closed Mondays)
Admission: Free
Address: Pembroke Street, OX1 1BP
Telephone: +44 (0)1865 722733
Website: www.modernartoxford.org.uk

8. Oxford University Press Museum

A small museum showing books and historic documents, as well as the live printing equipment of the Oxford University Press.

Opening Times: By appointment only for a 30 minute tour, between 10 and 4
Admission: Free
Address: Great Clarendon Street, OX2 6DP
Telephone: +44 (0)1865 353527

9. Museum of Oxford

A fascinating museum which celebrates the 'Town' rather than 'Gown' history of Oxford.

Opening Times: Tuesday – Friday 10–4, Saturday 10–5, Sunday 12–4. (Closed Mondays)
Admission: Free
Address: St Aldates, OX1 1DZ
Telephone: +44 (0)1865 252762
Website: www.museumofoxford.org.uk

10. Science Oxford Live

A hands-on museum devoted to the wonders of Science. Visitors are encouraged to engage with the.

Opening Times: Mon – Sat, 10–5. (Closed Sundays) Please call or check website to confirm opening times before visiting
Admission: £3 per person
Address: London Place, OX4 1BD
Telephone: +44 (0)1865 810000
Website: www.scienceoxfordlive.com

10 THINGS TO DO AROUND Oxford

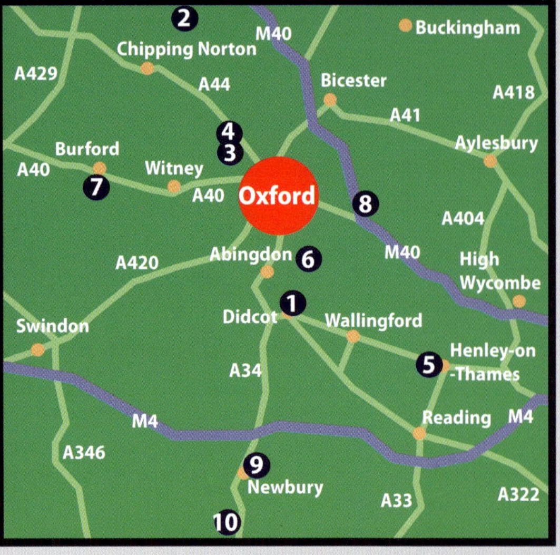

1. Didcot Steam Railway

Discover the engines of yesteryear with the chance of a trip on a steam train.

Opening Times: Weekends all year & daily opening in UK school hols. 10.30– 4 in Winter & 10.30–5 in Summer.=
Admission: Non-steam days: Adults £5, Concs. £4.50, Children £4. Variable on steam days and for special events
Address: Didcot, OX11 7NJ. **Tel:** 01235 817200
Website: www.didcotrailwaycentre.org.uk

2. Hook Norton Brewery

Founded over 150 years ago, this historic family brewery still upholds the tradition of using shire horses for its local deliveries. Tours with tasting are available.

Opening Times: Monday – Saturday 9.30– 4
Admission: £9.50 for tour (tour not suitable for those with walking difficulties, or under 12's; visitor centre only, free)
Address: Hook Norton, OX15 5NX. **Tel:** 01608 737210
Website: www.hooknortonbrewery.co.uk

3. The Oxfordshire Museum, Woodstock

The diversity of Oxford is celebrated in this interactive and award winning museum.

Opening Times: Tuesday – Saturday 10–5. Sundays and most Bank Holidays 10–3. Closed other Mondays (last admission 4.45)
Address: Woodstock, OX20 1SN. **Tel:** 01993 811456
Website: www.oxfordshire.gov.uk/the_oxfordshire_museum

4. Blenheim Palace

Often described as England's answer to Versailles, Blenheim Place is stunning landscape designed by Capability Brown.
Opening Times: Beginning November– end January open Wednesday – Sunday. All other months open daily. Palace & gardens 10.30–5.30
Admission: Palace, park and gardens from £18 per adult, £10 per child.
Address: Woodstock, OX20 1PX. **Tel:** 01993 811091
Website: www.blenheimpalace.com

5. Henley

Most famous for its July regatta, the bustling town of Henley is well worth a visit at any time of year. Antique shops, art galleries and fashion outlets will tempt your wallet, along with a huge variety of pubs and restaurants to suit all tastes.

Telephone: Henley Tourist Information 01491 578034
Website: www.visitsouthoxfordshire.co.uk

6. Harcourt Arboretum

Part of the Botanic Garden, The Arboretum is a magical place to visit at any time of year.

Opening Times: April to November, daily from 10–5 (last admission 4.15). December – March, Monday – Friday, 10–4.30
Admission: Adults £3, Concessions, £2.50
Address: Nuneham Courtenay, OX44 9PX. **Tel:** 01865 343501
Website: www.botanic-garden.ox.ac.uk

7. Cotswold Wildlife Park

Set within parkland and gardens around a listed Victorian Manor House, the Park is home to a fascinating collection of mammals, birds, reptiles and invertebrates.

Opening Times: Daily, 10–3.30 in Winter and 10–4.30 in Summer.
Admission: Adults, £11.50; Children & Concs, £8
Address: Burford, OX18 4JP. **Tel:** 01993 823006
Website: www.cotswoldwildlifepark.co.uk

8. Waterperry Gardens

Stroll around eight acres of magnificent gardens, explore the beautiful plant centre and indulge in retail therapy in the Garden Shop, Gallery, Gift Barn and Teashop.

Opening Times: Daily from 10–5 in Winter and 10–5.30 in Summer
Admission: Adults, £3.85; Children under 16, Free
Address: Nr. Wheatley, OX33 1JZ. **Tel:** 01844 339254
Website: www.waterperrygardens.co.uk

9. Newbury Racecourse

An exciting day out for all the family. Alongside regular horse racing fixtures, there is a children's nursery and an 1 8-hole golf course.

Opening Times: Year round, call or check website
Admission: Adults, from £15; Children under 18, Free (with the exception of certain party events)
Address: Newbury, RG14 7NZ. **Tel:** 01635 40015
Website: www.newbury-racecourse.co.uk

10. Highclere Castle

A stunning 17th century house with connections to the discovery of Tutankhamun's tomb. Explore the fascinating Egyptian exhibition within the atmospheric castle cellars.

Opening Times: July–September 11–4.30; closed in Winter. Call ahead for spring opening times
Admission: Adults, from £9; Concs. from £8; Children, from £5
Address: Newbury, RG20 9RN. **Tel:** 01635 253210
Website: www.highclerecastle.co.uk

Stranger Than Fiction!

Holywell Cemetery

Charles Dodgson, better known by his pen-name, Lewis Carroll, took inspiration for the fictional characters of Alice's Wonderland from the people he encountered in Oxford. One such man was Theophilus Carter, a cabinet maker who lived at number 49 High Street. Aside from his main business, Theophilus was an avid inventor, one of his more ingenious creations being the Alarm Clock Bed which, at the desired hour, would tilt and deposit its inhabitant into a bath of cold water! Theophilus was well know for eccentric behavior and would always wear a top hat, balanced on the back of his head. He was of course, the inspiration for the Mad Hatter. Theophilus is buried in Holywell Cemetery.

A Slip of the Tongue

The Reverend William Archibald Spooner (1844–1930), Warden of New College, Oxford, was notoriously prone to mishaps in his speech, switching corresponding vowels and consonants, often to comic effect. Best loved examples of his mispronunciations include "Is it kisstomary to cuss the bride?" (Is it customary to kiss the bride?), "Is the bean dizzy?" (Is the Dean busy?) and "You have hissed all my mystery lectures." (You have missed all my history lectures.).

The term 'spoonerism' has now made its way into the Oxford English dictionary.

New College

A Dangerous Occupation

Lovers of crime fiction will know Oxford as the home of one of the best loved sleuths of all time, *Inspector Morse*. With 33 episodes shown over 13 years, the television adaptation of Colin Dexter's novels became loved by millions for twisting plots set against the historic Oxford background. After Morse's death in an episode called *'Remorseful Day'*, the baton was taken up by Morse's sidekick, Lewis. Episodes of *Lewis* are still filmed around the streets and colleges of Oxford and you may well encounter a television film crew during your visit.

Life as a University Don in Colin Dexter's fictional Oxford is one fraught with danger. Eighty one Oxonians including three heads of colleges were killed off in his crime novels!

Morse died here in Exeter's Front Quad

Oars At Dawn!

Bumps Results

Rowing is a famous University sport and plays an important part in the rivalry between colleges and indeed, Universities. There are two annual rounds of "Bumps" in Oxford known as The Torpids and The Eights. The Bumps are inter-collegiate rowing contests which take place over the course of several days. The sport was devised for parts of the river too narrow for traditional racing. The teams' boats are spaced at 1.5 lengths apart along the river at the beginning of the race.

The object is to catch up with and 'bump' the boat in front and avoid being 'bumped' by the boat behind. At the end of the week's event, the team who has 'bumped' the most boats is crowned Head of The River.

Penicillin. The Miracle Cure.

The Penicillin Memorial

Whilst Alexander Fleming is most commonly associated with the discovery of penicillin, it was a team of Oxford scientists who succeeded in determining its use in medicine. The first person to be treated with penicillin was Albert Alexander, a reserve police constable in Oxford. In December 1940, Alexander received a scratch to his face from a rose thorn which quickly became infected with both Staphylococcus and Streptococcus. He was admitted to the Radcliffe Infirmary where his condition worsened. At the time, a team of scientists led by Dr Howard Walter Florey were experimenting with the medical applications of penicillin at the School of Pathology in Oxford. Until this point, they had only performed their experiments on mice and were fearful of its possible effects on humans. In order to perform a human trial, they required a patient already in a terminal condition. When they heard of Albert Alexander's condition, they decided that he was a suitable candidate for treatment. On 21st February, 1941, Alexander was given a 200mg dose of penicillin. Within just 24hrs, his temperature had dropped, he had regained his appetite and the infection had begun to improve. Tragically, due to shortages caused by wartime restrictions on Florey's laboratory, the available penicillin ran out within 5 days. Albert Alexander died on 15th March 1941. Despite the less than satisfactory outcome of this particular case, the results the team had witnessed proved that penicillin had no harmful effects.

Gruesome Gargoyles

One of Oxford's many grotesques

Gargoyles, or 'grotesques' as they are more correctly known (gargoyles feature water spouts), are an iconic feature of Oxford's architecture. As you explore the city, you will encounter leering faces, ferocious creatures and comical characters at almost every turn. The first recorded grotesques in Oxfordshire appeared around 1,000 years ago on Norman churches.

Whilst many within the city are centuries old, there are many much more recent examples too. In 2009, nine new grotesques were unveiled on the north-west face of the Bodleian. Designed by local children, these represent real and fictional characters associated with Oxford's history and include Thomas Bodley, Lewis Carroll's Tweedle Dum and Tweedle Dee and General Pitt Rivers.

Getting to and from Oxford

By train:

Oxford is linked to London by the Paddington to Oxford direct service, which runs every 30 minutes. There is also a direct service from Birmingham new Street. Additional services from the South are via Reading; and from the West via Didcot. For further details contact National Rail Enquiries on 08457 484950 (+207 278 5240 from abroad) or visit www.nationalrail.co.uk.

By bus:

The Oxford Express is a regular service between Oxford and London Victoria Coach Station. Journeys take approximately 1 hour 40 minutes and run at intervals of 30 minutes or less, 24hrs a day. Contact the Oxford Bus Company on 01865 785410 or visit www.oxfordbus.co.uk for more information. For information on coaches to other major cities and airports contact National Express on 08717 818178 or visit www.nationalexpress.com. Coaches arrive at Gloucester Green Coach Station in Oxford city centre.

By car:

Oxford is 62 miles northwest of London and takes around 1hr30mins by car. Oxford's road links to some main UK cities in brief:

From the East (London) via the M40
M40, junction 8: A40 to Oxford

From the Midlands via the M40
M40, junction 9: A34 to Oxford

From the West via the M4
M4, junction 15: A419 North, then A420 to Oxford

From the North via the M6
M6, junction 7: M42 southbound, junction 3a: M40 southbound, junction 9: A34 to Oxford

From the South via the M3
M3, junction 9: A34 to Oxford

By plane:

London Heathrow is the closest airport to Oxford, followed by London Gatwick. Road access from both is via the M25 and then M40 into Oxford. Both airports have regular bus services into the city.

Getting in and out of town

Park and Ride

Due to Oxford's limited parking facilities, we highly recommend the Park and Ride system. You can park your car for £1 (free at Thornhill and Water Eaton) and ride the bus to the city centre for £2.00 return, with up to 3 accompanied children under 16 free.

Buses run approximately every 10 minutes during the day Monday – Saturday from 6am–7.30pm (approx) and every 15 minutes 8.30am–7pm Sunday (approx).

Park and Ride depots can be found at the following 5 sites:

- **Peartree (to the north, off the A43). Bus no. 300**
- **Redbridge (to the south, off the A4142) Bus no.300**

Continued…

Whilst in town

Park and Ride *continued*

- **Seacroft (to the west, off the A34) Bus no. 400**
- **Thornhill (to the east, off the A40) Bus no. 400**
- **Water Eaton (on Banbury Road to the north of the city, ex. Sundays) Bus no. 500**

Car Parking

Parking within the city centre is limited, expensive and not recommended. If you choose to drive into the city, the biggest car park is the Westgate Shopping Centre. 1210 places. Pricing from £1.90 per hour NB includes shopmobility where battery operated wheelchairs can be borrowed free but must be pre booked on 01865 248737.

Tourist Information Centre:

Opening Times: Monday – Saturday 9–5, Sundays and Bank Holidays 10–4.
Address: 15–17 Broad Street, OX1 3AS
Telephone: 01865 252200
Website: www.visitoxford.org/tic

Post Office:

For useful things like money transfers and buying stamps, the main Post Office is located at 102-104 St Aldates, OX1 1ZY. The Post Office is open from 9–5.30 Monday to Saturday, closed on Sundays.

Banks:

There are banks with ATMs (cash points) located throughout the city. Those most conveniently located for the sightseeing trails are near the cross roads of Cornmarket/St Aldate's/High Street and Queen Street.

Public Toilets:

The following public toilets are marked on the town map. All listed below have access via the National Key Entry Scheme for disabled visitors and have baby changing facilities.

- **Market St (9–5pm plus overnight cubicle)**
- **Gloucester Green (9–5pm plus overnight cubicle)**
- **Westgate Car Park (9–5pm plus overnight cubicle)**
- **Speedwell St (March – October 9–5pm only)**

In an emergency

Hospital

We hope you don't need this during your stay, but just in case, Oxford's John Radcliffe Hospital is on Headley Way, Headington, OX3 9DU. The hospital has an A&E department.

Dial 999 in case of emergency to contact the police, fire brigade and ambulance service.

The police station is situated on St Aldates, OX1 1DB. Their local telephone number is 01865 266000.

Index